The Nüremberg Fünnel
Idaho-German Tales

by
George M. Klein

LEGENDARY PUBLISHING COMPANY
BOISE, IDAHO

Library of Congress Catalog Card Number: 96-076373
International Standard Book Number (ISBN): 1-887747-01-X

First Edition

Original illustrations by Forrest Christensen
Edited by Jean Terra
Design & Layout by Richard Terra/Terra Nova

Legendary Publishing Company
P.O. Box 7706
Boise, Idaho 83707-1706

Printed in the United States of America by
Thomson-Shore, Inc. – Dexter, Michigan

Preface

As the son and grandson of German immigrants, I was taught to stifle any show of emotion. It was no-nonsense with my father who believed "real men don't cry." A handshake was on the threshold of being too demonstrative. Pointed questions of a personal nature by children were discouraged. *Kinder* were excluded from conversations about family misfortunes or scandals.

I wish it had not been so. I also regret the anger and antagonism directed towards German immigrants during World War I that precluded the teaching of their native language to German-American children. In attempting to shield their children from the anti-German war hysteria, they spoke "Deutsch" only when they were alone or to share secrets, thus increasing their child's isolation.

Fortunately, neither my mother nor my grandmother fit the role of the harsh scolding *hausfrau*. Their love and good nature were constant. Through stories, song and prayer, they taught me to cherish life. They also taught: "Speak the truth."; "It's *verboten* to wallow in self-pity."; and "Prove you love me, clean up your plate!"

Nevertheless, I regard myself as sort of a "stiff neck" when it comes to the verbal expression of my emotions. For better or worse, writing has a way of liberating my inhibitions, restoring my memories, and activating my imagination.

This book of short stories — mostly true, some fabricated— is about myself, real people, and events that were important to me and significant in my life. It is with love and affection that I dedicate these tales as "Valentines" to my kinsfolk, friends, and all the characters herein, real or imagined.

George Matthew Klein
February, 1996

ACKNOWLEDGMENTS

I thank the many people who helped me write this book of short stories: Jean Terra, who by her patient and careful editing held the stories together; Lorry Roberts of Legendary Publishing Company, for providing her expertise; Valorie Taylor, Myrna Sasser, Jane W. Holt and Bethine Church, for sharing their memories of Verda Barnes; Mary Anne Solberg, Carmelita Spencer, Betty Lou Montell, Bill Bridge, and Eldene Wasem for their assistance with photographs from Idaho County.

I also wish to acknowledge my debt to my son Douglas Klein, my granddaughter Laura Klein-Duffin, and my sister-in-law Doris Klein for their help with research. And to friends Ronald Bush, Mammie Curtis, Louise Heth, Marjorie Koch, Lynda Clark, and Carolyn Frei, Editor of *Idaho County Voices*, for their sustaining moral support. To my sister Lucille Jones who inherited a wonderful German sense of humor, thinks I'm awful funny, and contributed a bundle of old family photos. To Forrest Christensen, illustrator *extraordinaire;* to the Special Collection Archives of Boise State University; to Jim Maguire and Arny Stov, Boise State University, editors of "Western Writers Series"; to Mildred Beckwith who provided information on John A. Beckwith, author of *Gem Minerals of Idaho;* to Gisela Burke for voice messages from Nüremberg, Germany.

To the Special Collections Section of the University of Idaho

Library as well as to Philip "Flip" Kleffner and James Lyle, director and former director respectively of the University of Idaho Alumni Association, for furnishing photos of interest. To Phil and Helen Hartley for the portrait of me on page 179. Both the North Dakota State Historical Society and the North Dakota State Tourism Department obliged by responding to my requests for information and photographs. To the Boise Public Library for their friendly and efficient service. To Teresa Brizendine of Shanandoe Enterprises who translated my scribbles into words.

And it goes without saying, to Elvera, author of *Creative Sourdough Recipes,* and my wife for sixty years, for her encouragement, patience and tolerance throughout the writing of this book and our lifetime together.

If my bad memory has missed anyone, I sincerely apologize.

G.M.K.

A Bit of the Past . . .

BICENTENNIAL HISTORICAL MUSEUM

305 N. COLLEGE   GRANGEVILLE, IDAHO 83530   (208) 983-2373

Established 1986 – Bicentennial Horizons Committee Inc.

"DANKE SCHÖN"

George Klein, former Mayor and civic leader of Grangeville, Idaho, has donated all receipts from the sale of his book *The Nüremberg Fünnel* to the Grangeville Bicentennial Historical Museum. The book contains several delightful stories about our town, its inhabitants and our history.

We appreciate this and all contributions for the maintenance and perpetuation of our museum.

Carmelita Spencer

Bicentennial Historical Museum
305 North College Street
Mailing address: Rt. 2, Box 500
Grangeville, Idaho 83530

To collect and preserve Idaho County History

TABLE OF CONTENTS

The Squeak from the Golden Gate

Some are called in the name of Alexander, and some for Hercules, or Hector and Lycurgus and such great names as these, but of all the world's brave heroes what is the gain to christen a wee man child Charlemagne?

Charlemagne Mendelssohn Braun was christened in 1913 at Saint Francis Catholic Church, San Francisco, California. His mother, Cleopatra Braun, was Captain of the "Hetchy-Hetchy," a ferry boat operating between San Francisco and Sausalito. She had worked her way up from deckhand to become the only woman officer in the San Francisco Ferry Boat Company fleet. Proud of her position, Cleopatra never shed her blue, gold-braided pants and coat or her visored cap with C-A-P-T-A-I-N embroidered in gold letters across the front. Sometimes, in her off hours, Cleopatra would stand at the ramp of Pier "B" in her splendid regalia basking in the admiration of the boarding passengers. Only when her trousers no longer fit around her plump pregnancy did she wear a dress.

Motherhood had little appeal to Cleopatra Braun. First Mate Vaughn La Rochelle joked, far out of Cleopatra's hearing, "Maybe she'll jus' put the little bugger in a dinghy and push him out to sea."

Pictured is one of the San Francisco Ferry Boat Company's fleet that criss-crossed the Bay on an hourly schedule between San Francisco, Sausalito, Oakland, Richmond and San Rafael. Most of these boats were docked in the 1930s when construction was completed on the Golden Gate and Oakland Bay Bridges.

From early childhood, Cleopatra Von Zurück had resolved to become captain of a sailing ship. While her friends where going to dances and parties, Cleopatra was on the docks talking to mariners. She had no time for landlubbers. Her father, a German immigrant, imported and sold Turkish rugs. He was troubled by his only child's fanatical love of the sea.

"What am I to do?" Siegfried Von Zurück wailed. "She won't listen to me. All the time down at the Embarcadero. I'm afraid for her. She should find a nice boy and get married."

But Cleopatra never altered her course and, in spite of his misgivings, Siegfried was proud of his daughter on the day she was commissioned and licensed as Master Navigator and Captain. Cleopatra was now fully qualified to command any vessel in the San Francisco Ferry Boat Company fleet.

Captain Cleopatra Von Zurück's reputation for efficiency, performance on the Bay, maneuvering smooth landings, and maintaining a clean, shipshape boat was widely known and greatly appreciated by management, crew, and passengers. When winter storms slashed through the Golden Gate, churning up twenty-foot white-top waves and bringing swirling winds and blinding rain, all amassed to assault her lumbering vessel, Captain Cleopatra relished the challenge. With nerves of steel, she piloted her craft through the tempest, past the warning buoys and hazardous guide pilings, smoothly lowering the drawbridge, and finally lashing the boat safely to the wharf. This was the life she loved; men and romance were out of the question — until the day she met Maximilian Rudolph Braun.

On the first Saturday of every August, the San Francisco and North Pacific Railroads, owner of the ferry boat service, held its annual employee picnic at dominant Mt. Tamalpais. Rising 2600 feet above sea level, the mountain top provided a view of the entire Bay Area. In 1912, remembering what a rotten time she had had the previous year, Cleopatra had decided not to attend the annual event. At the last minute, she changed her mind and joined the picnic party at Sausalito as they waited to board the narrow gauge railroad train that would puff its way up the steep grade for eight miles to the top of the mountain.

Advertised as the "Crookedest Railroad in the World," the Mill Valley and Mt. Tamalpais Line was hailed as the most unique of all mountain railroads. As a safety measure, the locomotive, named "Black Maria," pushed rather than pulled the train up the mountain and the number of passenger cars was limited to three. These primitive cars were open-sided with back-to-back, outward-facing seats, giving the sightseers an unobstructed and intimate view of the magnificent scenery.

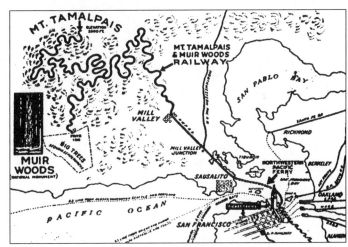

Map shows the "Crookedest Railroad in the World": the Mill Valley and Mt. Tamalpais Line running to the northwest of San Francisco.

Active promotion by the owners of the Mt. Tamalpais-Muir Woods Railroad had local residents and tourists flocking to take a ride on the mountain train. The fare was very reasonable, only $1 for the round trip. The ride up the mountain took about an hour and slightly less than that for the coast back down.

The passenger cars were open-sided with back-to-back, outward-facing seats, giving the sightseers an unobstructed and intimate view of the magnificent scenery. The locomotives pulling the trains can be seen on the switchbacks behind the passenger cars. Upon reaching the summit, the trains stopped at the "Tavern of Tamalpais," a

first-class dining establishment at the resort hotel where scores of visitors from the States and abroad spent their vacations. Roads and motor cars ended the brief life (from 1886 to 1929) of the little railroad, but hikers can still enjoy the spectacular scenery by walking the old railroad right-of-way to the summit.

Sophie Robrecht and Eugene DuPree below the lookout on Mt. Tamalpais, California, February 12, 1905.

Cleopatra, an experienced rider of the "Crookedest Railroad," took a seat next to one of the vertical handrails that would provide her with a steadying hold as the little train steamed and puffed up the steep grade, leaning, lurching and wiggling around the sharp curves.

The conductor had already called out "A—L—L—A—B—O—A—R—D" when a young man with a heavy German accent addressed her saying, "Hello, please could it be *'gestalten'* to *'sitzen'?"*

"Sure," Cleopatra responded. "This is a free country. You can *'sitzen'* wherever you damn please."

The young German was not with the ferry boat crowd. He was on a sight-seeing trip on his day off from Ringling Brothers Circus. A talented trapeze artist, he had suffered a disastrous mishap that had sent him crashing forty feet to the ground, breaking both his ankles and legs. His recovery was slow and he had lost his nerve for the high bars. His employers, wanting to give him time to regain his confidence, had hired him on as roustabout until the end of the season, the last week in October.

Handsome, muscular, and well dressed, the German was about seven years Cleopatra's junior. She liked younger men, saying, "They are more impressed with my status and easier to manage than older guys."

It was almost love at first sight. Before the little train reached the top of Mt. Tamalpais, Maximilian Rudolph Braun had won the fickle heart of Captain Cleopatra Von Zurück. Only three days after their meeting on Mt. Tamalpais, the young lovers prevailed upon the circus chaplain to unite them in holy matrimony. The short ceremony was witnessed by the trick horseback rider, two clowns, and three trapeze artists.

The newlyweds spent their honeymoon in Maximilian's circus quarters, a little room closed off from the Pullman-like railroad car by a green curtain and with a bright red curtain at the window. It was furnished with shelves of books, pictures of Maximilian's family in Germany and two young women he identified as his sisters, plus four bottles of champagne and two dozen roses. After three days alone, sustained only by frequent toasting of champagne, Maximilian and Cleopatra finally emerged into the world of reality and practicality.

On November 1, 1600 performers, workman and hundreds of animals were scheduled to board their assigned sections of the train that would transport the entire circus to its winter quarters in Florida. The circus business manager agreed to grant Maximilian a month's leave providing he reported to the winter headquarters on December 1 at his own expense.

Until her marriage, Cleopatra had been living in a boarding house for young working girls. She and Maximilian couldn't live there — and now the circus train was getting ready to take their honeymoon home off to Florida. Cleopatra's parents were furious that she had not told them she was getting married. Worse, she had not been married in the Catholic church! She was destined for hell! Siegfried Von Zurück slammed the door in his daughter's face when she asked to move back home with her new husband.

With just one hour to change into her uniform and report to the "Hetchy-Hetchy," Cleopatra was beginning to panic. In her curt, commanding 'Captain's' voice she told Maximilian, "You got us in this mess, now go and find us a suitable place to live. Get my things at the boarding house and meet me at Pier 'A' at exactly 11 p.m. Don't you dare be late!"

Maximilian was astonished. His mouth dropped open, his eyes grew round, he was speechless. German wives didn't talk like that to their husbands! Besides, he had no money to pay for lodging and he was too proud to ask Cleopatra for anything. For two hours Maximilian sat smoking his pipe thinking about what to do. Finally, he looked at his watch and saw that he had just enough time to catch the circus train before it departed for Florida. "To hell mit it," he said and off he went to join his circus companions, leaving his new bride behind.

Cleopatra was concerned when her husband failed to meet her at Pier 'A' as she had directed him to do. It took her a while to realize that he wasn't going to show up and that in all likelihood, she would never see Maximilian Rudolph Braun again.

Three months later, Cleopatra confessed to her parents that she was going to have a baby and that her husband had abandoned her. They forgave all and insisted she move back home so they could help her raise the child. After the birth of her son who was given the names Charlemagne Mendelssohn by his grandfather, Cleopatra demonstrated no real love or affection for the infant and left all his care and rearing to her parents. Nor did she display any remorse or longing for the child's father. Ringling Brothers Circus returned to the Bay Area every year but not once did Cleopatra go looking for Maximilian or inquire as to his whereabouts.

Siegfried Von Zurück had a library filled with books on early and medieval Mediterranean history. Mere mention of the Ottoman Empire, the Holy Roman Empire, or the Crusaders, provided an opening for him to deliver a dissertation covering the history of Asia and the entire European continent. He alone bore full responsibility for the names he bestowed upon his only daughter and her child.

Charlemagne Mendelssohn Braun's first namesake was his grandfather's hero, King of the Holy Roman Empire (neither very holy nor Roman) who, in the eighth century, created the foundation of modern Europe. The second name was in honor of Felix Mendelssohn, a musical genius and conductor-composer of the nineteenth century.

Sister Mary Blanche, Charlemagne's kindergarten teacher at Saint Augustine's School, kept a sharp eye on the aggressive Braun child who was responsible for most of her discipline problems. Once he had even caused her to completely lose control when he plunged both his hands into the goldfish bowl sending the bowl, fish, and water crashing to the floor. "You little . . . . ," Sister Blanche said before regaining the tolerance, patience, and love that went with her calling. Repenting, she said, "Charlemagne is much too pretentious a name for a child. We'll just call you Charlie."

The name stuck and with the new name came the dawn of a new personality for the Braun boy. His grandfather finally agreed that the moniker "Charlemagne" was a handicap. Just plain "Charles" put him on a more even footing with his peers. The child's behavior improved and his grandmother, recognizing the improvement in her grandson's deportment, decided, "Yes, he's a Charlie!"

The nation was suffering through the Great Depression at the time Charlie graduated from Saint Ignatius High School. Jobs and money were scarce but the young man was eager for his independence. Father O'Connor, his school advisor, told him, "Charlie, this is a good time to go to college. Get more education so you'll be qualified to get a good job when the economy improves."

Charlie agreed but he had saved only $317 from his paper route and odd jobs. Father O'Connor helped him figure out a solution. Low tuition, cheap subsistence, accreditation, and prospects for part-time employment were the important considerations in his choice of a college to attend. Finally, Charlie decided that the University of Idaho was his best bet. The small university, located at Moscow in the northern part of the state, met all his criteria and it was far enough from the Bay Area to get him out from under his grandfather's dogmatic discipline.

It was a time of economic panic and troubled migration by hoards of unemployed men seeking jobs, riding the rails, hitching rides on vehicles, or driving their families to wherever there was a chance of work. Resisting his grandmother's pleading for him to stay home and with suitcase in hand, Charlie headed north on U. S. Highway 1.

It was more than 800 miles to the Palouse Country, as the

area around Moscow, Idaho, was known. Charlie made the trip in five days, hitching rides all the way. Sometimes he could ride all night with a kindly trucker. When he found himself stranded at nightfall, he slept along the road, in haystacks, or on park benches.

No one, neither his fellow university students nor his instructors had to ask, "Where are you from, Charlie?" Everyone on campus acquainted with Charlie Braun knew the freshman was from California. He was consumed with the notion that "it was his inalienable right and responsibility to boost the virtues of the Golden State!" Only the benevolence and academic tolerance of the faculty and the leniency of the student body allowed Charlie to live through his freshman year. Admonished for his excessive promotion of his native state, he would unabashedly respond, "Guess you never been there."

Charlie conformed to all the University's customs and edicts including wearing the traditional freshman's green cap called "the beanie." He never missed a major sporting event and was an enthusiastic organizer of the annual bonfire-rally preceding the football game between the University of Idaho and Washington State College. Charlie's dress on these occasions was not the foremost in collegiate style for the northern climate. He wore a yellow oilcloth raincoat, known as a "slicker," rubber and canvas galoshes (unbuckled), tan corduroy trousers, and the ubiquitous green "beanie."

It was the fad on campus to paint colorful cartoons and absurd one-liners on the back of slickers. J. P. Brown, Charlie's roommate at Lindley Hall, had the words "O Tempora! O Mores!" printed in blazing red and illustrated by a leering devil on the back of his slicker. Without Charlie's consent, J. P. painted Charlie's slicker with a map of California and the words "Toast-and-Jam Charlie — the Squeak from the Golden Gate." The residents of Lindley Hall thought it was a great joke on the brassy freshman and they were disappointed when Charlie reacted with delight, expressing enthusiastic thanks to J. P. for the art work.

9

Tradition mandated that Freshmen wear green beenies to separate them from superior upperclassmen in the 1930s. Administration Building in the background. Historical Photo Collection #1-52-32, University of Idaho Library, Moscow, Idaho.

The Freshman Bonfire was a campus tradition in the 1920s and '30s, and outhouses were prime fuel. Historical Photo Collection #2-102-6b, University of Idaho Library, Moscow, Idaho.

Charlie wore his slicker with pride. The "Toast-and-Jam" nickname was a reference to his gluttonous appetite. At 6-foot 3-inches and weighing 145 pounds, the California beanpole never missed a meal. It was particularly exciting to witness the manner in which he quickly disposed of his breakfast. Stacks of toast and jars of jam were the first to go, followed by whatever was within his reach. Charlie's remarkable appetite was exceeded only by his relentless enthusiasm for his native state.

Charlie had a hard time explaining why he had come to Idaho. He had several pre-packaged answers depending on his audience. Often he claimed it was pre-ordained. If the question came from a good-looking coed, he said, "When I was a little kid my grandmother sang a song about Idaho that I never forgot." If the young lady was naive enough to ask him to sing the song, he would croon:

"Way out west in Idaho,
There's a gal that I love so
Ida, my Idahoo!
Racing across the prairie,
I keep singing the refrain.
Ida don't go so fast, dear,
My horse won't last, dear,
So please go slow.
Ida, my Idahoo!"

After the song, his punch line was, "I had no idea where Idaho was but to me, the picture of racing a horse across a prairie with a girl named Ida was wonderful. That's why I love Idaho girls." Charlie thought it was a perfect line and he never could understand why he had so much trouble getting dates.

Every Sunday evening, Charlie and his fellow residents of Lindley Hall gathered in the basement dining room for a "smoker." It was only one of thousands of such gatherings in universities across America. Some suggested the "smoker" was invented by the tobacco industry; others claimed its origin was the Native American Indian practice of passing the peace pipe at a pow-wow. The university students didn't pass the peace pipe but free sample packs of Lucky Strikes or Camel cigarettes were always available and they were encouraged to "light up." How could the collegians refuse?

The glamour of tobacco was vaunted by movie stars. The silver screen was clouded with cigarette smoke. The radio, newspapers, periodicals and billboards across the land proclaimed the social virtues and sophistication of smokers. Particularly attractive to young macho males was the "Blow Some My Way" billboard showing a beautiful woman imploring a debonair gentleman to exhale his cigarette smoke in her direction. That was long before the Marlboro Man but it was even more effective.

The "smoker" was strictly a male event. The entertainment might be boxing, magic tricks, dancing girls, or ad lib audience participation. At Lindley Hall, on the University of Idaho campus, it was mostly the latter. Charlie was always eager to perform. He sang "Way Out West in Idaho" and accompanied himself by strumming on his second-hand five-string banjo, a gift from Father O'Connor. He had a voice like a crow and even though he had first explained how much the song meant to him, he was booted off the platform before he finished the ditty.

Three weeks later the hard-shelled Californian was back to give a recital of his favorite poem — the only poem he knew. He had been required to memorize it in honor of Columbus Day, a red-letter day at Saint Ignatius High and a patron's day for the Catholic men's society, Knights of Columbus.

Charlie was preceded on the "smoker" entertainment agenda by Donald Murphy, another extrovert freshman from California. He always got a big hand for his imitation of the radio newscaster Walter Winchell and his trademark "Good Evening, Mister and Mrs. America and All the Ships at Sea."

It was a hard act to follow, but Charlie stepped up to the platform paying no attention to the groans and hisses. Was this nut going to try to sing again? "Where's your banjo, Charlie?" Charlie was oblivious to the harassment. Politely he requested the audience's attention.

Very poised and sincere, Charlie introduced himself and smoothly began to tell the story of Joaquin Miller, California's great "Poet of the Sierras." Born in Indiana in 1841, he was christened Cincinnati Hiner Miller but later changed his name to Joaquin — here, Charlie recognized a common bond.

Joaquin Miller lived a life filled with exciting travels and adventure; he was an Indian fighter, a pony express rider, gold prospector, lawyer, judge, teacher, nomad and author. To many people, he portrayed the very spirit of the western pioneer. The tales of his loose morals, cavorting with Indians in northern California, and defying the law were overlooked by the religious.

From 1887 until his death in 1913, Miller established himself as a sort of a messianic guru of the Oakland Hills, where he had purchased 75 bare acres overlooking San Francisco Bay. There he built his home, *The Abbey*, entertained famous writers and wrote his best known works. He also planted an astonishing

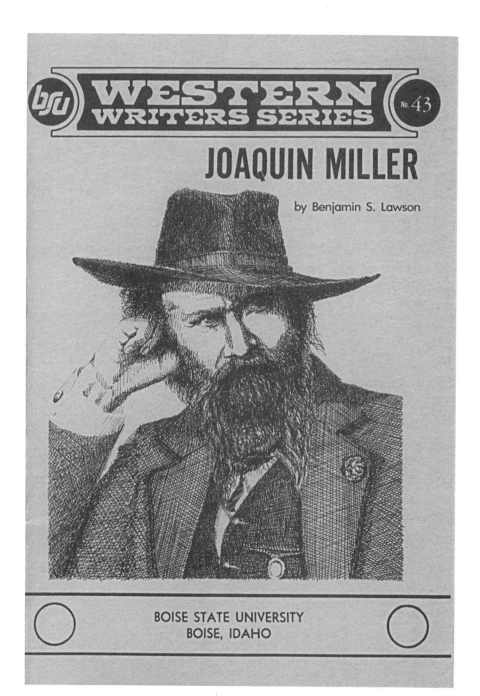

WESTERN WRITERS SERIES

No. 43

JOAQUIN MILLER

by Benjamin S. Lawson

BOISE STATE UNIVERSITY
BOISE, IDAHO

Joaquin Miller, California's great "Poet of the Sierras." Miller lived a life filled with exciting travels and adventure: Indian fighter, a pony express rider, gold prospector, lawyer, judge, teacher, nomad and author. To many people, he portrayed the very spirit of the western pioneer. Illustration courtesy of the Western Writers Series, Boise State University.

75,000 Monterey pines, cypress, olive and the first eucalyptus trees in California.

Charlie described his own visit to Miller's retreat in the Oakland Hills saying, "Although he died the year I was born, I have always had great affection for Joaquin Miller's works. I have been to his cherished home where he built monuments to Robert Browning, Moses, and John C. Fremont with his own hands and, as a child, I was present when his daughter Juanita gave beautiful readings of her father's poems."

Charlie paused. He was pleased to see that his fellow "smokers" were listening to his introductory remarks so he proceeded to recite, without script, Joaquin Miller's best known poem "Columbus."

Behind him lay the gray Azores,
Behind the Gates of Hercules;
Before him not the ghost of shores;
Before him only shoreless seas.
The good mate said: "Now must we pray,
For lo! the very stars are gone,
Brave Adm'r'l speak; what shall I say?"
"Why, say: 'Sail on! Sail on! and on!'"

"My men grow mutinous day by day,
My men grow ghastly, wan and weak."
The stout mate thought of home; a spray
Of salt wave washed his swarthy cheek.
"What shall I say, brave Adm'r'l, say,
If we sight naught but seas at dawn?"
"Why, you shall say at break of day:
'Sail on! Sail on! Sail on! and on!'"

They sailed and sailed, as winds might blow,
Until at last the blanched mate said:
"Why, now not even God would know
Should I and all my men fall dead.
These very winds forget their way,

For God from these dread seas is gone.
Now speak, brave Adm'r'l, speak and say—"
He said: "Sail on! Sail on! and on!"

They sailed. They sailed. Then spoke the mate:
"This mad sea shows his teeth tonight.
He curls his lip, he lies in wait,
He lifts his teeth, as if to bite!
Brave Adm'r'l, say but one good word:
What shall we do when hope is gone?"
The words leapt like a leaping sword:
"Sail on! Sail on! Sail on! and on!"

Then pale and worn, he paced his deck,
And peered through darkness. Ah that night
Of all dark nights! And then a speck—
A light! A light! At last a light!
It grew, a starlit flag unfurled!
It grew to be Time's burst of dawn.
He gained a world; he gave that world
Its grandest lesson: "On! Sail on!"

Charlie wasn't prepared for the warm approval to his reading — especially when, after the first verse, the audience joined him chorusing "Sail on! Sail on! and On!"

The applause was music to Charlie's ears. He was delighted when the hall proctor, Professor John Beckwith, who taught Western Literature, congratulated him on his rendition. Charlie was in Professor Beckwith's "bonehead" English class because he had flunked the English entrance test. He was "a damn poor speller" and his grandfather had blamed the nuns for teaching him phonetics. Charlie had provided his classmates at St. Ignatius with some great laughs whenever he attempted to compete in a "spelling bee." On one notable occasion, he was asked to spell cougar. "That's easy," said Charlie, sounding out each syllable, "koo-ger — k-o-o-g-e-r."

"Wrong," said the teacher. "Well," said Charlie, "if it don't

16

spell kooger, what does it spell?" After that, the Parochial School System sort of gave up on teaching Charlie to spell.

Professor Beckwith was a good teacher and a patient man. He never spoke at the "smokers" unless things got rowdy or the presentations got ridiculous. But Charlie's story and poem by Joaquin Miller moved Professor Beckwith to comment further on the little known exploits of the "Poet of the Sierras" in central Idaho.

He said that Charlie's talk was "the first real educational presentation we have had at these 'smokers' and I want to thank Charlie for making it entertaining."

Professor Beckwith continued, "With your indulgence, I would like to add to the story. Did you know Joaquin Miller was a prospector and pioneer in Idaho, and was part of the state's early history? Yes, some of you from the Salmon River country have heard of the old mining town of Florence. In 1861, the settlement was known as Millersburg for Joaquin Miller who took out the first panful of dirt that yielded $25 worth of gold. When word of

John Beckwith, Graduate Gemologist with an M.A. in English, taught at the University of Idaho and for 20 years at Boise State University. He lectured throughout Idaho on gemology and is author of Gem Minerals of Idaho *with Field Trip Maps. Photo courtesy of Mildred Beckwith.*

Miller's find reached the newspapers, prospectors came pouring into Idaho's remote wilderness from all over the world."

A hand went up, "How much gold did they find?" Professor Beckwith responded, "I'd guess about $25 million in gold."

He said Joaquin Miller had written: "The wheat-like grains of gold were there, and in such heaps as had never been found in California; and so accessible, only a few inches under the turf or peat in the little meadows and little blind gulches here and there in this great black, bleak, and wintry basin that had never yet been peopled since it came fresh from the Creator's hand."

The Professor continued, "Miller had the sense to leave with his rich find before heavy snows and sub-zero temperature trapped hundreds of miners. For many, the lust for gold was stronger than reality and they stayed on their claims only to die of exposure or starvation."

John Beckwith, English professor, was also a serious collector of native gems. He studied the geological location of Idaho mineral deposits and the early history of its mining towns. He later wrote and published *Gem Minerals of Idaho* — complete with field trip maps.

Professor Beckwith's knowledge of Joaquin Miller amazed Charlie. "Joaquin Miller was in Idaho? I never heard that before. What a nifty story. I can hardly believe it!"

"There's more, Charlie," said the English teacher. "Joaquin Miller claimed that his friend Colonel Craig had said that a peculiar arched light over the mountain south of Lapwai, Idaho, was called E-dah-ho — meaning 'light on the mountains' — by the Indians. Later, in his chronicle of 1899, Miller contradicted his first story saying it was the Indian name for 'bright object falling from the skies.' In 1923, the *Lewiston Tribune* called it 'The light that never was' because of the many conflicting stories of the origin of the name Idaho."

Charlie's ego was at a new high. To think that the "Squeak from the Golden Gate" was responsible for what Professor Beckwith termed the most intellectual "smoker—bullfest" he had ever attended! Charlie gained confidence from his performance but he was having trouble with his grades and was losing inter-

Boxing became an intercollegiate sport under Coach Louis August, who vaulted the University boxers into national prominence in the 1930s. Historical Photo Collection #2-125-33, University of Idaho Library, Moscow, Idaho.

est in his classes. Moreover, he was low on money and ready to quit the University.

That all changed the day Louie August, his boxing instructor in Physical Education, matched him with 5-foot 4-inch Henry Zimminsky from Pierce, Idaho. Tough, and built like a Jack Pine stump, Henry landed two rights to Charlie's ear, one hard left to his jaw and it was "lights out" for Charlie Braun!

Zimminsky retired happily to his corner of the ring. "I guess I gave ole Charlie what-for. Maybe I knocked California out of him for a while." But when Charlie didn't get up and the coach, kneeling beside the vanquished boxer, called for the campus doctor, Henry regretted decking his opponent.

Charlie lay in the University infirmary for three days in a deep coma. The word on campus was that "Charlie Braun was going to croak from the beating he took from Henry Zimminsky." University President M. Gordon Neile, the faculty, and the Administration were in distress and reports on the patient's condition were issued hourly to the press and to Idaho's Governor C. Ben Ross.

Charlie's roommate, J. P. Brown, said, "I think Charlie's playing possum and loving all that attention."

Meanwhile, a benevolent plot was being hatched concerning the comatose student. Doctor Henrietta Josephine Trumanhauser, the German language teacher, telephoned the infirmary to inquire about Charlie. "Is it possible for me to talk to the boy?" she asked.

"Talk to him all you want, Doctor, but that boy is out cold," Charlie's nurse responded.

The Great Depression of the 1930s was a difficult financial time for most students. As many as 80 percent of the University of Idaho's students held jobs on and off campus. Charlie Braun worked for the Student Civil Works Program and at Scott's Greenhouse. His friends, the Kurdy Kids — Helen, Kelly, Tom, John, Tony and Frankie — had grown up on a farm not far from Grangeville. They devised many ingenious ways to make their way through college. Besides transporting most of their subsistence from the family farm, they converted an old garage close to the campus into very livable quarters. They also did very well selling meat produced on their farm to the campus dormitories and fraternity houses.

Many students lived in or near poverty but most regarded their condition as part of the essential struggle for an education. People in every walk of life were financially crippled by the depression but many citizens of Moscow, including University faculty, came to the rescue when "the wolf was at a student's door."

Doctor Henrietta Josephine Trumanhauser, known as the "Idaho Angel of Mercy," was one of the good Samaritans to poor students. She tried to keep her good works a secret but the tall, thin woman in the Mother Hubbard dress was often recognized

The Kurdy Children: George, Kelly, Tony, Frank, Tom, John, Mary and Helen, from Greencreek, Idaho, in March, 1941. Seventeen Kurdys from first to third generation are U of I graduates. Photo courtesy of Tom Kurdy.

as she was leaving a box of groceries, a bundle of clothes, or an envelope of money at the door of a needy student. Sometimes she left a little unsigned note: "I like to see students struggle but I don't like to see them starve."

Although she never admitted it, Madam Trumanhauser, as she liked her students to call her rather than Fraulein Trumanhauser, was selective of those upon whom she bestowed her charity. She had access to the transcripts of the students and it simply made sense to her to help those with good scholastic records.

Madam Trumanhauser had trouble locating Charlie's records because there was no one at the University registered as "Charlie Braun." She did find a Braun but it was Charlemagne Mendelssohn Braun. She decided, "This must be it but I can't

"Angel of Mercy," woman of compassion and gracious lady, Madam Doctor Professor Henrietta Josephine Trumanhauser, Language Department, University of Idaho. Photo courtesy U of I Alumni Association.

understand how he has passed himself off on everyone as a 'Charlie.'"

Madam Trumanhauser was disturbed about this deception and concluded, "The boy is suffering from chronic eccentricity. He is denying his great namesakes and I must help him find his lost identity."

When Doctor Trumanhauser entered the infirmary vestibule, the nurse was expecting her and said, "Yes, Doctor, he was still comatose until about seven o'clock. Then, he started stirring and talking crazy. I couldn't catch most of the words except that he repeated over and over 'Sale on, sale on.'"

Charlie carefully opened one eye, then the other, and tried to find some familiar object in the Spartan infirmary room. The buzz in his brain, coupled with numbness in his neck and the nausea in his stomach, made him aware that something dreadful had happened to him.

Gosh, am I going to die, he thought. There must be someone around who could tell him. He saw a little cowbell on the stand next to the bed. With considerable effort he reached out with his left hand, gave it a couple of shakes and dropped it on the floor. Immediately, the door flew open and the very professional Nurse Hamilton followed by Madam Doctor Trumanhauser burst into the room. Neither of the women spoke. They looked at Charlie who was too ill and bewildered by his situation to say anything.

Nurse Hamilton felt Charlie's forehead, took his pulse count, turned to the German Professor and said, "Doctor, it looks as though our little patient is going to be okay. All he needs now is a lot of rest and nourishment. Too bad rules won't allow us to keep him here more than five days. He just can't go back to the dormitory in his condition."

"Yes," Doctor Trumanhauser said, "concussions must be taken very seriously or permanent brain damage is possible."

Charlie understood the conversation but said nothing because neither of the women had addressed him. Also, he was afraid that he was in trouble for something he may have done and now couldn't remember. As the sedatives he had been given once again took hold, his anxiety gradually subsided and a welcome drowsiness lulled him back to heavy sleep. Charlie was oblivious to the plan the two women were framing for his future.

Charlie was surprised, but too weak to care, when he awoke in new and unusual surroundings. He was lying on a short-legged army cot that was centered in a carpeted room. Except for the double doors, two heavily draped windows, and one painting in a gilded frame, the walls of the room were lined entirely with ceiling-high bookshelves and each shelf was completely crammed with books.

Charlie detected a faint odor of burned toast reminding him of the emptiness in his stomach. Still disoriented, he studied the painting in the gilded frame that hung on the wall across from the foot of his bed. The picture measured 3-feet by 5-feet and showed a bespectacled professor holding a funnel to a boy's head pouring something from a bottle marked "Knowledge" into the boy's brain. Charlie thought maybe he was hallucinating.

No one had as yet informed him of the circumstances leading to his condition and present situation but he was beginning to piece things together. He recalled the sting of Henry Zimminsky's glove when it connected with his left ear but nothing after that. Craving food and with an immense curiosity about his whereabouts, he tried to get up from the cot but found he was too feeble. Dropping back on the pillow, Charlie once again dozed off.

Doctor Trumanhauser was in her kitchen making toast and explaining to another woman about the boy on the cot in the library. "I don't know what we are in for," she was saying, "but I couldn't just put that poor boy in the hospital. The University won't commit to pay the bill and he has no money."

Hilda Alexanderson had been Henrietta Trumanhauser's housekeeper for sixteen years and nothing the generous woman did surprised her.

"Well it's alright with me, Doctor," Hilda replied, "but you know I got to be home to get Oscar's supper by five o'clock. Look there, your toast is burning!"

"Quick To Get Wise"

The "Nürnberger Trichter" glorifies the teaching talents of the Nürnberg schools and universities.

For centuries, Nüremberg, Germany — Nürnberg is an alternate spelling of the city name — has been the economic, cultural and academic center of Bavaria. This cartoon pokes fun at the learning process — the old professor funneling knowledge into the head of the young scholar. A capricious cure for ignorance. The origin of this illustration on a postcard has been lost in antiquity.

Doctor Trumanhauser pulled the toast off the burner, spread butter and jam on it and placed it on a tray with a glass of cold milk. "He hasn't had anything to eat except liquids since he was knocked out and Professor Beckwith told me he favors toast and jam. Maybe he's ready for this."

Quietly she opened the library door and set the tray of food on a chair beside the cot where Charlie was dozing. When the aroma of the fresh-burned toast made contact with the sleeping boy's nose there was an instant awakening. Charlie flung back the covers, swung out his legs, sat up, put the tray in his lap, and devoured the food.

Madam Trumanhauser was impressed, "My goodness that was wonderful. I'm so pleased you are recovering."

Charlie looked up at her. "Thanks, Madam, for the food. Do I know you? Are you my doctor? Where am I?"

Madam Trumanhauser explained to Charlie all that had happened since he had been knocked out by Henry Zimminsky, including the decision to move him to her home from the infirmary instead of to the city hospital.

"Your doctor has agreed that I can care for you until you recover enough to go back to Lindley Hall which should be in about a week. In the meantime, you are to rest and eat to regain your strength. My spare bedroom is filled with books so we put you in my library."

Charlie was beginning to feel woozy. He thanked Madam Trumanhauser for her kindness and lay back on the cot, puzzled. "Wow! A bedroom full of books so she puts me in her library?"

For the next five days, Madam Trumanhauser brought Charlie his breakfast and supper. She stayed to discuss all manner of subjects with him. At first, Charlie felt uncomfortable in the presence of this noble, highly educated woman who talked to him of the great leaders of the world — past and present. As she spoke of herself and her childhood in Nüremberg, Germany, the great old castle of Emperor Frederick Barbarossa, and the town hall decorated with paintings by Nüremberg's great artist, Albrecht Dürer, she revealed her love for the city of her birth. Charlie could relate to this and he was tempted to tell her about

San Francisco but he fought off the impulse.

Charlie was really amused when Madam Trumanhauser pointed to the painting in the gilded frame on the library wall and said, "See there, Charlie, that's how we educate young people in Nüremberg. They just make a little hole in the top of your head and with a funnel they pour in all the knowledge."

"What is the inscription across the top of the painting?" Charlie asked.

"Oh, I forgot you don't read German. It says, 'The Nüremberger Fünnel'."

Charlie laughed, "I wish it was that easy to learn here. Maybe you could fill my empty head with knowledge."

Charlie knew Madam Trumanhauser was serious when she took his hand in hers and said, "Charles, I may not be able to pour instant knowledge into your head but I know that you have the brains and qualities to be a leader. Professor Beckwith has told me of your performance at the 'smoker' and I have seen your transcript. You must not conceal your true name, Charlemagne. Your namesake was a great and powerful Emperor of the Holy Roman Empire, ruling most of Europe as we know it today. You must reclaim your true name and prepare for the destiny that awaits you!"

Charlie was flabbergasted. So she knew his name! He realized he had already made himself the subject of ridicule by relentlessly bragging about California. Did Madam Trumanhauser intend that he should compound his social errors by taking back his real name? He could just see the fellows in Lindley Hall bend over with laughter when they heard that Charlie Braun's real name was *Charlemagne!*

Each day, Charlie grew stronger. He continued to have edifying talks with Madam Trumanhauser about his future. Mostly, she talked and he listened. She constantly urged him to identify himself by his real name and prepare himself physically and mentally to honor his great namesake. Her obsession with the notion was beginning to have an influence on Charlie.

"Madam," he said, "if I do call myself by my real name, how can I avoid the ridicule of the Lindley guys?"

"That's easy," she said. "I'll start by calling you Charlemagne. Then, next semester you enroll in the school of law. Knowledge of the law is essential to every leader so you should start there. I know of many law students with marvelous names. You'll meet Kramer McKinley DeMars, Paris Chaunsey Cromwell, Homer Redlingshafer Reubke and Frederick Ludwig Aufderhinie. They are all nice boys and very smart."

Charlemagne decided Madam was right. Becoming a great leader fit his dreams of fame and future adventure. Perhaps he would emulate the first Charlemagne. Or maybe Joaquin Miller who was a lawyer and had also had an adventurous career with the Indians.

When Charlemagne reported to the campus infirmary, he was given a complete physical, pronounced well, and cleared to resume his classes and move back to Lindley Hall. He was sorry to leave Madam Trumanhauser's home but she invited him to come by whenever he could. He resolved to do so because he had developed a deep affection for the gracious lady.

Charlie said nothing to the fellows at Lindley Hall about his change of name or his plans to move the following semester. In fun, they called him "Boom Boom Braun." The second "Boom," they joked, was Charlie hitting the floor. Henry Zimminsky said he was sorry about hitting him so hard but then spoiled his apology by saying, "I thought you California guys could take a punch."

Charlie got a summer job with the U. S. Forest Service. From now on, school was going to be more expensive. Law students wore suits to class and he bought two new ones at David's Department Store.

The new and confident Charlemagne was no longer the braggart from California. His contributions to the "bullfests" were now about his experiences on Boulder Creek in the Saint Joe Forest — how the old logger Jesse Bodie could keep a wad of "snuss" (snuff) under his lower lip all night without spitting; about the time the chipmunks got into the flour barrel and the guys thought the hard stuff in their bread was raisins; or when some of the crew escaped from a black bear with two cubs.

When the Fall semester rolled around, Charlemagne Mendelssohn Braun registered in the School of Law. After paying for his books, tuition, and a deposit on a room at Ridenbaugh Hall, he was left with just $75.43.

You could spot the aspiring lawyers in their dark suits with vest and tie. Across his vest, Charlemagne wore an imitation gold watch chain attached to a large "Waltham" timepiece given to him by his grandfather. He was dazzled by his own elegance.

The Law School was devoid of females. Charlemagne had met a few "good lookers" at the Blue Bucket but, like a true son of his mother Cleopatra, he preferred to date younger high school girls because "they really appreciate my intelligence and maturity."

Charlemagne was down to his last dollar when he found a job that accommodated his class schedule and paid enough to cover his expenses. Professor John Beckwith had recommended him for the job of night watchman at the Joe Zeb Pea and Lentil Warehouse. The job was boring but Charlemagne could study while he protected the premises from thefts and fire. Fortunately, he never encountered either. Once, he inadvertently set off the burglar alarm and, not knowing how to turn it off, sprayed the device with the fire extinguisher. When the retardant shorted

Administration Building, University of Idaho.

the alarm, it stopped. He was docked a week's pay to cover the damage.

"Charlemagne Mendelssohn Braun!" President Neile called out loud and clear from the podium. Charlemagne paused, letting the full weight of the name fall on the ears of the graduation assembly. Not until Charlemagne reached for his diploma did the President emit the words, "Doctor of Jurisprudence."

The polite applause that followed sounded to Charlemagne like a roar of adulation and, deep in his heart, he attributed his accomplishment to his dear benefactor, Madam Trumanhauser. She had provided moral support, financial assistance, and wise counsel. When he was at wit's end to find a provocative subject for his thesis, it was she who suggested: "A History of the Law of Equity and Recent Court Decisions Relating to Its Application in the Forty-Eight States and Territories of the United States of America."

During the Great Depression, the majority of the University's students held jobs on and off campus. Below: A student Civil Works Administration (CWA) crew in the U of I Arboretum, 1933. Historical Photo Collection #6-8-2, University of Idaho Library, Moscow, Idaho.

The Daily Idahonian included C. M. Braun on the list of those passing the Idaho Bar and soon after, the new lawyer mysteriously departed Moscow without notifying anyone of where he was headed. A classmate later reported that Charlemagne had married a sixteen-year-old high school girl and was practicing law in Tetonia, Idaho.

Madam Trumanhauser pretty much confirmed this rumor when she said, "Yes, he's down there someplace. I don't know what's gotten into that boy. Last Christmas, I got a card with a picture of him and some young girl. They were both stark naked, hugging each other. I can't believe it. They were wearing Santa Claus hats. The greeting read, 'Best Wishes from Charlemagne and Rosa Braun — Jackson Hole, Wyoming.'"

Madam was very perplexed and said, "I hope he's not gone crazy!"

In 1941, Pendleton Howard, Dean of the school of law received a letter from the War Department, Office of the Advocate General, requesting a transcript of the scholastic record of Charlemagne Mendelssohn Braun. Lucille Thompson, the Dean's secretary, was told to obtain the records from the Registrar's office and send them on to the War Department.

Registrar Ellen Oleson was disconcerted when she saw the amount of paperwork this would entail. "Do they expect us to answer all these questions?" she asked. "We have never had a request like this before. I know of several law school graduates who are in the Advocate General's Department. We didn't have to go through anything like this for them."

Miss Thompson replied, "Maybe they are going to make him a General or something."

"More likely they suspect him of being a German spy," responded the Registrar, "with a name like Charlemagne Mendelssohn Braun! I remember that boy when he was sneaking around trying to hide his identity."

Major Braun was well regarded by his superiors in the Advocate General's Department in Washington, D. C. His job, reviewing records of General Court Martial decisions from military courts for all theaters of war, kept him behind a desk. Several times he requested a transfer to the European theater but each time, it was denied.

His subordinate, Captain Hajimi Hohri, said the General was probably doing Major Braun a favor. "The Germans probably would have shot him as a traitor if he was captured — with name tags reading 'Charlemagne Mendelssohn Braun'."

On May 7, 1945, the Germans signed the unconditional surrender. Two weeks later, Major Braun received orders to report for duty at Reims, France. Notice of his promotion to Lieutenant Colonel reached him two days after reporting to the Allied Joint Delegation for the Unconditional Surrender of the Germans. He missed the ceremonial signing but he headed the task force responsible for "scrutinizing the multinational surrender document for errors and omissions."

Most members of the detail, including a few civilian linguists, were disgruntled with the work. Lieutenant Colonel Braun was the first to voice his complaint, "What the hell are they going to do about these nit-picking spelling errors? Start the war again?"

On July 4, 1945, Lt. Colonel Braun packed his gear and, with two enlisted military police, traveled by jeep to Nüremberg, Germany, where they were to report to the "International Military Tribunal for the Trials of Nazi War Criminals."

Colonel Braun was glad to have the company of the two armed Military Policemen. To avoid uncleared land mines, Braun and his escort drove the marked road that connected the towns and villages. For the first time, he witnessed the cruel aftermath of modern warfare.

"Alles Kaput." He remembered his grandmother using the expression when he had smashed her precious antique demijohn. *"Alles Kaput,"* he said to himself as each spectacle of devastation came into view.

Here and there, Germans were scrounging through the wreckage, perhaps searching for their dead, looking for their possessions, or trying to reconstruct their homes. No one except the children looked up or acknowledged their passing. The German kids, recognizing the U. S. Jeep, ran after them hollering, "Hey Joe! Give me chocolate!"

Charlemagne was suffering from a splitting headache when the jeep finally pulled up in front of the "International Military Tribunal" in Nüremberg. The hard eighteen-hour ride through the demolished and ravaged land had left Lt. Colonel Braun sick, tired and cranky. He would be happy to return to the United States immediately — a post-war casualty, critically wounded just by witnessing the devastation of the war.

His weariness and gloom dissipated after ten hours of undisturbed sleep. Charlemagne could adapt quickly to any new environment. His private quarters were clean, the mess was tolerable, the joint allied command was well organized. He was pleased to be part of this solemn military tribunal and ready for his assignment:

"Lieutenant Colonel Charlemagne Mendelssohn Braun, U.S.A., 02145, Report to Room 3, Tribunal Headquarters, 22:00 Hours, 21 July, 1945, for Briefing and Assignment."

The briefing, conducted in four languages, was a bore. During a welcome break, Colonel Braun complained to the British Captain in charge, "I can't understand what they are talking about, and what I *should* understand, I can't hear."

The Brit, tapping his pipe on the ashtray, replied, "Beg your pardon. What did you say?"

The American responded, "The hell with it!"

Fortunately Colonel Braun's written instructions were intelligible and clear. As the senior in grade officer of the United States Army, he would head the Allies' team for the prosecution of Hans Fritzsche for war crimes according to the rules of the Geneva Convention on Criminal Acts of War.

The portfolio of Hans Fritzsche was pretty thin for a Nazi War Criminal. Colonel Braun had expected he would be prosecuting one of the big fish like Herman Goering; he could put his heart into hanging that rat!

Hans Fritzsche was only a small-fry official in the German Propaganda Ministry and a radio announcer. Other than that, there was little evidence to link him to the murder of innocent women and children, the Holocaust, or the inhuman treatment of unarmed prisoners of war. Hans wondered why he was there. Colonel Braun could find no reason why Hans was there and he was acquitted.

Major Paul Joseph Petain, the French member of the accusers, was disappointed. He was ready to hang all Germans. On the side, he told the others, "I think that Colonel Charlemagne Mendelssohn Braun is a Nazi sympathizer."

The Colonel, tired of attempts to distort the truth, told the press, "Fritzsche was acquitted because he is innocent of the charges brought against him. I'm not disappointed. No, I did not permit false witnesses to testify. My job was to see that justice was served and I'm glad it's over. I'll be going stateside tomorrow."

James Lyle, the congenial Alumni Secretary of the University of Idaho, was on the phone to Madam Doctor Henrietta Josephine Trumanhauser, "Yes Madam Trumanhauser, this is Jim Lyle. . . . Yes, I'm Alumni Secretary now. . . . Yes, I do enjoy the job very much. . . . Yes, Madam, I called to see if you have an address for Charlemagne Mendelssohn Braun. . . . Yes, we sent it there but the mail returns. . . . Thank you Madam."

Jim was puzzled. He didn't know where to turn next. It seemed that the "Squeak from the Golden Gate" had dropped completely off the map.

The Idaho football team was scheduled to play the University of North Dakota at Grand Forks and Jim had arranged a pre-game alumni luncheon at the old General Custer Hotel. The Idaho Alums at the luncheon were few in number and Jim was becoming concerned about the sparseness of the crowd when he heard someone say, "Look, isn't that Charlemagne Braun over there?" Jim turned to look. Sure enough, there was old "Toast-and-Jam" Charlie.

"What a surprise," Jim greeted Charlemagne like a long-lost brother. He liked the guy. Jim liked everybody. "Why, you old devil," he said to Charlemagne. "We've been looking everywhere for you."

Jim proceeded to pump the truant alum for information on his location and activities since the war. Charlemagne was pleased with all the attention and when Jim invited him to say a few words about himself he characteristically over-obliged. But it was game time and the wordy attorney was left talking to himself. Jim regretted having to leave his old classmate but he was riding to the game with one of the guests and had to go. Anyway, he had all the information he needed for the next issue of the *Idaho Alumni Roundup* newsletter.

Name:	Charlemagne Mendelssohn Braun, Attorney at Law
Home Address:	429 Emperor Barbarossa Lane Bismarck, North Dakota
Business:	Suite 31, Von Hindenberg Building Bismarck, North Dakota
Marital Status:	Divorced, one child

Bismarck, North Dakota, the Capital since statehood, was named for the "Iron Chancellor" of Germany in 1873. The founders wanted to induce German capital and attract German immigration. Charlemagne was quite at home in the city with its Bavarian-style culture mixed with a strong Native American presence. He was twice elected State President of the American Civil Liberties Union, served on the Commission for Indian Affairs, Council to the Allied Tribes Pow-Wow Committee, and Director of the State Square Dancing Association.

Attorney Charlemagne Braun rated high on the State Speakers Roster as a knowledgeable and entertaining speaker on a wide range of subjects. Some audiences, however, complained that he was too long-winded and repetitious. But that didn't stop Charlemagne from repeatedly telling his favorite old saw:

"Once when Bismarck was a brawling boom town, a newspaper editor inquired about a subscriber's family and was told that the man's father had died.

'Got shot did he?' asked the editor, who also wrote the obituaries.

Left: Signboard advertising the Patterson Hotel. Photo courtesy of the North Dakota Historical Society.

Right: Bismarck's Patterson Hotel, an historical landmark and past social center. Photo courtesy of the North Dakota Historical Society.

James Lyle (left), Past Executive Secretary of the University of Idaho Alumni Association, and his successor, Flip Kleffner, at Jim's 90th birthday party. Photo courtesy of the U of I Alumni Association.

The subscriber shook his head.

'Drank too much whiskey?'

The man shook his head again.

'Well, he can't be dead then,' said the editor, 'because that's the only way men die in Bismarck.'"

Charlemagne often altered the story to fit the circumstances or the occasion. He did wonders with it when he told it to a medical convention or the Alcohol Beverage Distributors.

In October 1977, Charlemagne was guest speaker at the Allied Tribes Pow-Wow Committee's annual business banquet at the Bismarck Patterson Hotel. The articulate attorney was a real friend to the tribes. Many times he had provided legal services to them "pro-bono publico" on difficult claims involving treaty rights. He was one of the leading defenders of the Oglala Sioux Tribe who on February 27, 1973, signed the Settlement at Wounded Knee, South Dakota, in protest of conditions on the Pine Ridge Reservation. The government's prosecution of the active Indian participants and the Whites who attempted to supply the Tribe under siege was under the infamous Rap Brown Act. Charlemagne reminded people everywhere of the countless crimes against the Indian people. He scolded officials in Washington, D. C.:

"In 1890 the United States Army killed 300 unarmed Indian people at Wounded Knee. Are we no better today in our treatment of these indigenous people? We have massacred them, tormented them, stolen their land, purged their culture. Why did this mighty nation, founded on the principles of Thomas Jefferson and asserting life, liberty and pursuit of happiness to all peoples, stoop so low at Wounded Knee? Have we learned nothing? Must we respond to a cry for help from a desperate impoverished tribe by bringing against them the full force of the government's modern arsenal?"

All banquets of the Allied Tribes were preceded by a press conference. The meeting with the press and television reporters was useful as a public relations tool. It was also an incentive for the members to get to the meeting on time. Great emphasis was placed on the time scheduled for the television interviews. The invitation read: "SEE YOU ON TV!" As everyone enjoyed being seen on television, it helped spur punctuality and the station cooperated.

Perennial Chairman Black Eagle said, "Before we baited the hook with possible television exposure there was no one here until ten or eleven o'clock. Indian people say, 'Happy bird takes no account of time.'"

Charlemagne Braun had learned to adapt to "Indian Time" and was surprised to find everyone already eating at nine o'clock when he took his guest speaker's place at the table next to Chairman Black Eagle.

That morning, when Charlemagne's secretary, Edna Morning Star, had opened the office mail, she found that it included the most recent issue of "Vital Speeches of the Day." Ordinarily, she would simply have dropped the publication in the lawyer's "IN" basket but the title, "Columbus, Hero or Villain?" caught her attention. After reading the speech by Donald J. Senese, former Assistant Secretary of Education, she had carefully propped the publication against the face of Charlemagne's desk clock. He found it almost immediately.

Charlemagne was troubled by the broad insinuation made in the speech that native people were condemning Christopher Columbus as "a Renaissance Darth Vader who ushered in five centuries of imperialism, raping and butchering the native Caris who greeted his 1492 voyage."

This description angered the liberal lawyer. Charlemagne's role model was Joaquin Miller. Miller's greatest poem, "Columbus," in which he venerated the tenacity of the adventurous mariner, was a literary tribute to the Genovese explorer.

"It is nonsensical for Native Americans to make a scapegoat out of Christopher Columbus," Charlemagne said to Edna. "Is this the age of 'the anti-hero' where no one is really great and we have to put everyone under a microscope to check every imperfection, true or imagined? Must we try to debunk all national or personal heroes? What about George Washington, Abraham Lincoln, Chief Joseph, Sacajawea, Sitting Bull, Pocahontas and Joaquin Miller? — to name just a few."

Charlemagne told Edna he was thinking about making the subject the theme of his talk to the Pow-Wow Committee banquet. Edna Morning Star was frequently the captive audience to Charlemagne's tirades and often gave him back more than she took. Now, she advised him, "Put a lid on it Char!"

Everyone in the Indian Community and many Whites were aware of the special relationship between the lawyer and his secretary but they didn't "beat the drums" about it. Many years ago, Charlemagne had gone to Fort Yates, North Dakota, to take a deposition from a witness in an insurance claim. While there, he fell in love-at-first-sight with a beautiful 16-year-old, the granddaughter of the witness, Mrs. Loretta Redfeather.

The naive young girl, flattered by the advances of the city lawyer, was easy prey to his wooing. Charlemagne showered her with lavish gifts and when she discovered she was going to have a child by him, he immediately proposed marriage. Discord prevailed when Mrs. Loretta Redfeather pronounced that there would be no marriage of her granddaughter Edna Morning Star to the city lawyer whom she called "Big Wind That Speaks."

"Is it because he is a white man?" the granddaughter questioned through her tears.

"No, that has nothing to do with it," Mrs. Redfeather replied.

"Then, what?"

"First place, you're too young to marry. Second place, he's a big windbag lawyer who chases after young girls and drops them as soon as they show a little age; and, third, neither of you is psychologically mature or realistic enough to get married."

"What about the baby, Grandmother?"

"The baby will be born here on the Standing Rock Reservation, and become a member of the great Sioux Nation. That's how it will be!"

But that was not the end of it. The baby, a girl who was named Charlotta after her father, stayed on the reservation but the young mother was sent to college at Grand Forks when she finished high school.

Charlemagne kept track of Edna and whenever he was between marriages, he proposed to her. She, being a smart practi-

Photo courtesy of the North Dakota Historical Society.

cal child of her grandmother, always turned him down. She admitted she did like him but only as a friend who took her to fine places to eat and sent her money for college.

When Edna completed her paralegal studies, Charlemagne offered her a good-paying and interesting job in his office. Her boyfriend, Angus McCormick, said, "You know, I'll lose you if you go to work for that shyster."

Edna, convinced her affection for Charlemagne was now purely platonic, told Angus, "He's no shyster. You've got to believe me — it's all over between Char and me and the pay is great! Maybe you should ask me to marry you instead of being jealous of Char!" Angus agreed and the two were married.

Edna had now worked for Charlemagne for ten years and she enjoyed the work. She confided to Angus that she thought the old attorney was now impotent. "It's been two years since he divorced Fern, his last wife, and he hasn't made a pass at me. Maybe that's why he's getting so eccentric."

Edna thought Charlemagne's outburst about Columbus was evidence of his growing senility. He promised her that he would not mention the "Columbus thing" in his talk at the Allied Tribes Pow-Wow banquet that night but after three screw drivers at the hotel bar, all promises were off. Charlemagne decided that the Allied Tribes should hear his defense of Christopher Columbus.

The audience was polite and attentive when he was introduced. In their hearts, they had hoped it would be very short speech but now the white guy was reciting a poem about Columbus. "Sail on! Sail on! Sail on!"

When he finished the poem, Charlemagne talked about the recent harsh criticism of Columbus by some Native Americans and how unjust the attack had been when measured against the facts.

He quoted Donald Senese: "Columbus was a genuine hero. He won praise for his religiosity, his commitment, his ideals, his determination, and for his accomplishments."

By then, the people in the rear of the room who weren't completely asleep were nodding but Charlemagne continued his praise of Columbus:

"He is a model for all races, for men and women who can adopt these traits and apply them to their own lives. History is made by a series of events, some good, some bad, and in viewing history, we have the advantage of hindsight. Could we have done a better job if we had been in charge? What about slavery? Even among Indian tribes, it is now condemned universally.

"Every day, I see American Indian people who shrink from conflict and confrontation and who suffer through the most outrageous charges, allowing these attacks to go unanswered in the name of peace and harmony. Too often your silence is viewed as consent and thus gives credibility to the 'Big Lie.' Indian people should understand the values in other cultures without disparaging their own great culture and their brave tribal heroes. Christopher Columbus was a *genuine* hero in an *age* of heroes!"

The applause was mild yet Charlemagne felt he had delivered one of his better speeches. Indian folks are usually not very demonstrative so the lawyer was amused when one of the young activist men, Crow Bird, threw it back in his face. "C. M. Braun gave a speech to members of the Allied Tribes Pow-Wow Committee," he wrote in his letter to the editor, "and he defended Christopher Columbus, the Italian who butchered native people in his hunt for gold and claimed he found America when we were already here. C. M. Braun is a racist polecat in sheep's skin."

Edna reproached Charlemagne. "You promised me you would not mention Columbus in your talk to the Allied Tribes

Pow-Wow Committee. I told you that Columbus stuff doesn't sell around here."

"Honestly, Char," Edna continued, "you are the most bull-headed, God-damnedest, know-it-all, Caucasian, egotistical male in the world! You've been bleeding over this Columbus guy since I first knew you. Indigenous people have their bellies full of that ruthless bastard."

Charlemagne was disturbed by Edna's tirade but he took it without comment — which further infuriated her. Long ago, Charlemagne had learned the futility of arguing with Edna when she was on the War Path. Fortunately for him her outbursts were few and far between.

The next day, Edna told her husband Angus about the incident and that she was sorry for her angry words. She admitted that she knew what Char's reaction would be after he read Donald Senese's speech. She had pushed it on him, deliberately set him up.

"Apology" was not a word in Edna's vocabulary but Angus convinced her she should make amends.

It had been almost two months since they had visited Edna's people at the Standing Rock Reservation. Her grandmother, Mrs. Loretta Redfeather, had passed her eightieth birthday but was still in fair health. Edna's bi-racial daughter, Charlotta, was still in Mrs. Redfeather's charge. The young girl had a deep affection for her great-grandmother but now, growing into her teens, Charlotta was manifesting signs of early maturity. She wanted to move to the city to be with her mother. Edna had not pressed the subject because she felt time would soon resolve the matter.

Edna was eager to visit her family and she knew Charlemagne was as anxious as she was to see their beautiful daughter. He had told her of driving down to Fort Yates by himself some time ago and of being rudely treated by Mrs. Redfeather and Edna's brothers. They had directed him to leave and to stay away from Charlotta.

Charlemagne was delighted when Edna and Angus invited him to accompany them on their trip to the reservation. Surely, he thought, he would receive a better reception if he was in their

Jesse "Jay" Taken Alive, Past Tribal Chairman, expresses his philosophy on a sign at the entrance to the reservation. Photo courtesy of the North Dakota Historical Society.

company.

It was a wonderful visit. Charlemagne was treated cordially by Mrs. Redfeather and Charlotta proved to be a fascinating child, smart and with a joyful disposition. She knew Charlemagne was her natural father and she expressed her love for all three of the visitors. Before they left the little unpainted house in the Standing Rock Reservation, Charlemagne was already making plans for Charlotta's future.

Columbus was "on hold" and Edna was forgiven.

For two months James Lyle, University of Idaho Alumni Association Executive, had been trying to begin a countrywide exploratory trip to establish Alumni Chapters in as many states as possible. His departure from Moscow had been postponed twelve times because the congenial man couldn't say 'no' to appeals for favors, personal or business. Finally, in August 1983, he took the phone off the hook, left the mail unopened and departed his office to visit Alumni in as many states as he could in the time allowed him.

Third on his list of places to visit was Bismarck, North Dakota. There, the "Alum" to see was Charlemagne Mendelssohn

Braun, class of 1936. The two men sat in the cocktail lounge of the Bismarck Patterson Hotel for five hours talking about old and new times. They also drew up an organizational list for an Idaho Alumni Chapter for North Dakota. Several other local Idaho Alums joined them late in the evening.

Jim was enthused at the response, "Gosh, Charlemagne, this was great. Do you suppose you can come to Moscow in 1986? It will be our 50-year reunion and you will be amazed at the growth of the University since you left."

The idea appealed to the lawyer. "Sure, send me the information and I'll try to make it," he said.

In May of 1986, Charlemagne and his daughter Charlotta set out for Idaho. They had a rough flight in the small plane and a rocky landing on the Pullman-Moscow airport. Charlotta, usually in good spirits said, "Where are we Dad? Someplace in Siberia?"

Charlemagne was still reeling from the flight and had an upset stomach. He said, "Maybe we are but I'm not getting on that plane again."

Jim Lyle didn't recognize the couple at first glance. Charlemagne now had a long gray beard and he was wearing a buckskin leather jacket with fringes on the sleeves, Tillman cowboy boots, a wide-brim Stetson hat, and dark glasses.

He looks more like Buffalo Bill than Charlemagne, Jim laughed to himself. He couldn't place the slender, good-looking, dark-skinned woman with him but, remembering Charlemagne's reputation for wooing young women, he thought it might be a new wife.

Charlemagne and Charlotta spotted Jim waving to them as they approached the small airport building. Charlemagne was happy to see his old college friend and Charlotta was glad to see anyone who would drive them to civilization (which was remarkable for a girl born and raised on the Standing Rock Indian Reservation).

As they drove the nine miles to Moscow, the men kept up a steady stream of conversation paying no attention to the young lady in the back seat. Then, Jim remembered and turned his head slightly toward the back seat and said, "Are you from Bismarck too?"

"Oh pardon me," said Charlemagne. "I forgot to introduce you. Jim, this is Charlotta — Charlotta, this is Jim."

Jim didn't know who Charlotta was or why she was here and he was too polite to ask. He drove on to the University Inn where Charlemagne had reservations, helped unload the luggage, and accompanied the visitors to the registration desk. Only then did he understand the relationship between the two when the young woman was given a key to her own room, thanked Jim for the ride, and turned to Charlemagne, saying, "I'll see you later, Dad. Call my room when you're ready to go eat."

So Charlotta was Charlemagne's daughter! The old rascal never told me he had a daughter, thought Jim, and she is something!

Charlemagne would have enjoyed more time for visiting and reminiscing with his classmates but the agenda was paced at a fast gallop. The Golden Reunion Anniversary Alums, all over seventy years of age, were pressed to keep the pace. Without his daughter's help, the Bismarck attorney would have missed the buses taking them to the planned events. Charlotta explained to Will Overguard, driver of one of the buses, "Dad never met a person he didn't like to talk to, especially if it is about himself."

Charlotta accompanied her father on all the tours and to all the dinners, banquets, and entertainment. She was at ease in the amiable environment of the Moscow campus. She was no stranger to academia and her only moment of irritation came at the University President's Reception when a faculty wife asked her if she were an Idaho student. Charlotta politely explained, "No, I am here with my father who is attending his Fiftieth Reunion."

"And where are you going to school, dear?" Normally, Charlotta would pass such a question off but the woman was so patronizing, she said, "I just graduated from the Massachusetts Institute of Technology in Aeromechanics and in two weeks I'm going to Wichita, Kansas, where I have a job with Boeing Aircraft Company."

The woman was startled by the curt answer, "Oh my! Isn't that incredible."

The daughter of all the Sioux had suffered similar insulting remarks. "Are you calling me a liar? Go ask my Dad, he's right there in the buckskin jacket."

The woman backed off. From a place of safety, she whispered to her husband, "Who *is* that girl over there?"

On the one open evening of the reunion, John Kurdy, a friend of Charlemagne's from Grangeville, Idaho, invited the two Brauns, Weldon Shmike, Bud Murphy, Russ and Ilene Horzowski, and Boyd Marlin to join him for dinner at the Elks Club. Fortunately, their table was in a small private dining room. Inhibitions fell away, the generous glasses were filled and re-filled with wine, everyone talked at once — it was a great party. Over the stern objections of his daughter, Charlemagne recited the poem "Columbus" with the rest of the party joining in on the chorus of "Sail on! Sail On!"

He also tried to recite Robert W. Service's "The Shooting of Dangerous Dan McGrew" but he had forgotten the second verse and Weldon Shmike had to finish it.

The next morning at breakfast, Charlemagne told his daughter he felt terrible.

"You shouldn't drink so much Dad," she said. "It's not good for your health. You should see yourself when you're drinking. You act like a braying donkey."

Charlemagne was accustomed to being told what to do and what not to do by Sioux women. All he wanted was a little sym-pathy. He should have known he wouldn't get it from Charlotta.

Jim had invited the father and daughter to come to his home that morning to meet his wife, Joyce, and daughter, Faye. It was nice to sit and visit in the quiet of the Lyles' pleasant living room. Faye was only a few months older than Charlotta and it didn't take long for the two career-bound young women to find many fields of mutual interest to talk about. Jim overhead his daugh-ter asking their young guest if she had a steady boyfriend. He cocked his good ear to hear the answer, "Well, not yet," replied Charlotta. "I like younger men. They are much more interesting and easier to manipulate."

Well, the acorns don't fall far from the tree, Jim thought to himself.

The final event of the reunion was the joint banquet for classes of 1936, 1956, and 1976. The speaker was the distinguished new University President Dorothy Zimmerman. The banquet room was too small for a sit-down dinner. The tables were jammed together. It was hot and stuffy and there was no one to take Charlemagne's order for a drink. He knew his daughter, who seemed to be enjoying herself, would not get him one. It was so noisy Charlemagne couldn't hear himself think and suddenly, he became uncomfortable, irritable, and downright unpleasant. He had to get out of this place. This was an important evening and he knew he was about to blow it but there was no turning back.

There was one thing Charlemagne had come here to do before he left this reunion. He pushed his chair back, stood up and worked his way through the tangled web of tables, chairs, legs and feet to the head table. "President Zimmerman. President Zimmerman !" He got her attention.

"I'd appreciate it if you would call for order here because I've got something important to say and then I've got to leave because it's getting awfully uncomfortable for me in this place and I've got to get outside."

Those sitting near President Zimmerman heard him and thought it was a hoax. After reading his name tag and trusting that Charlemagne really did have something important to say, President Zimmerman called for order, introduced the lawyer from Bismarck, North Dakota, and gave him the floor. She had no idea what the great announcement would be but hoped for the best.

"My dear Idaho Alums and President Zimmerman. I'm sorry to interrupt all this good conversation but I'll try to be brief." He paused and looked into the faces of the diners just as he would if addressing a jury. Seeing that he had their attention, he continued.

"When I came to this campus fifty-five years ago, I was a

green, dumb kid from California who thought he was smart. Besides being dumb, I was penniless — in the period of the Great Depression when you could actually buy something with a penny, if you had one. This University, the faculty, and the people of this town reached out to help me find my way, spiritually, academically, and financially. I am beholden to so many, some of whom are in this room tonight, that I will name only those I cannot thank in person because I waited too long and they are gone."

The waiters were starting to push through the doors with the long-awaited food but Flip Kleffner, Jim Lyle's designated successor, sensing something significant was about to happen, held them at bay, waiting for a signal from the head table.

Charlemagne was saying, "I want to thank Joe Zeb who gave me a job; John Beckwith, my proctor and English teacher who, among other things, almost taught me to spell and did help me get a job; Dean French, who taught me table manners and proper conduct; and my dear friend and principal benefactor, Madam Doctor Henrietta Josephine Trumanhauser, who raised me up from the depths of ignorance and despair, showed me the way to learn and live, and gave me the confidence and will to do it."

His voice starting to quiver, Charlemagne reached into his pocket and pulled out a white envelope, pronouncing with flourish, "President Zimmerman, I hereby tender you my check in the sum of $200,000 for the Madam Doctor Henrietta Josephine Trumanhauser Memorial Scholarship. Thank you all for your kindness in hearing me out. God bless all!"

The moment of silence that followed was all the time President Zimmerman needed to collect her thoughts. "Mr. Braun, on behalf of those present, the Board of Regents, the faculty and students of the University of Idaho, I gratefully accept this check for (oh, let me see it again), yes, $200,000 in memory of . . .," she paused. The name had escaped her and Charlemagne repeated it and spelled it out.

"I'll just say Doctor Trumanhauser," President Zimmerman continued. "This is a wonderful surprise. What a generous gift! It is a profound testimonial to this University's dedication to

University of Idaho Class of 1936, 50 Year Reunion, May 2–3, 1986

Front Row (left to right):
Ralph Samson, Ethel (Philips)
Longhurst, Mildred (Carson)
Schuldt, John Beck, Aurrel
(Laxton) Coughlan, Glenn
Coughlan
Second Row: Eileen (Kennedy)
Honsowetz, Ermel (Mattson)
Cordon, Alma (Almquist)
Martin, Dorothy (Preuss) Lee,
Frank Keyes, Hugh Eldridge,
Lewis Nelson, Edwin Nurmi,
Elva (Anderson) Clayton, Wayne
Hill, Don Petersen
Third Row: Margaret
(Brodecht) Conklin, Mildred
(Elliott) Fraley, Wendell Dayton,
Jay McDowell, Betty (Bandelin)
Black, D. Mark Hegsted, Keith
McDaniel, John Kurdy, Erick
Steiniger, Edward Lotovik
Fourth Row: Tom Burnam,
Harvey Nelson, Jerry Fogle,
George Turner, Rod Hansen, Bill
McCrea, William Hunter,
Frances Newton, Alf Dunn,
Horace Shipman
Back Row: Edgar Renfrew, Ken
Crawford, John Crowe, George
Klein, Frank Bevington, Wayne
Harper, Bill Teed, Glenn Owen,
John Aram, Russ Honsowetz

*Photo courtesy of the University
of Idaho Alumni Association.*

academic excellence and its commitment to sustaining a faculty that inspires, nurtures and cares about the potential of individual students. We all thank you, Mr. Braun, for the money and for making this a very special evening."

Charlemagne savored the kudos that followed. He had been carrying that check around since he had arrived in Moscow and, several times, he had experienced second thoughts about the gift.

Perhaps he would have been tempted to stop payment on the check had he heard some of the uncharitable remarks made by a few locals about his generosity.

"What absolute tacky theater," Mable Sources whispered to her sister, Leona. "These lawyers can't do anything without making it a big production."

Leona, who was as good at character assassination as her sister, replied, "Yes, and that getup, with the beard and all — I don't believe Dean French or anyone else taught him how to dress. Do you think that really is his daughter?"

But Charlemagne remained oblivious to these mean-spirited comments. Now, he felt good. His irritability about the banquet room was gone and he stayed to bask in the glory of the praise for his generosity.

Charlemagne was in good humor when he awoke the next morning. He was trimming his beard and humming "Here We Have Idaho" when the phone rang. It was Charlotta.

"Dad, are you dressed yet?" She didn't wait for an answer. "I called the car rental agency and they'll be sending a car over about nine o'clock so I'll meet you in the coffee shop in fifteen minutes. That will give us time to check out and be on our way to the airport. Got it?"

She didn't give Charlemagne time to confirm her instructions. "Damn," he said to himself, "she's starting to act like she's my parent instead of my daughter." But he complied with her instructions and soon they were on their way to Spokane, Washington, via Coeur d'Alene, Idaho. Charlemagne had convinced his daughter that this was the most scenic route.

For twenty miles north of Moscow, U.S. Highway 95 follows the foothill terrain of the Palouse Mountain Range. Charlemagne relaxed while Charlotta, guided by his directions, drove the rented minivan at a speed far lower than the posted speed limit. When Charlemagne noticed the string of cars behind them, he urged her to "Step on it! How come you're going so slow?"

"You know, Dad, I haven't been here before," she replied. "I don't want to miss anything."

Of course, it was absolutely taboo for Charlotta to confess her inexperience and admit her timidity about driving narrow, winding mountain roads. Also, she felt the presence of the tall evergreen trees crowding the roadway. She imagined their dark shadows were spirits blocking and blurring her vision.

Sensing his daughter's apprehension, Charlemagne said nothing more until they approached DeSmet where the open terrain revealed a small Indian settlement surrounded by farmland. Then, he told her they had entered the reservation of the Coeur d'Alene Tribe. "You will be driving through Indian lands for about forty miles. The next town is Tensed. That's DeSmet spelled backwards."

Having now achieved more than thirty miles of driving experience on the mountain highway, Charlotta had finally regained her composure. "How do you figure that? There's no 'm' in 'Tensed'."

Charlemagne was perplexed. "Now, why did you go and spoil that delusion for me? You don't know how many people I've told that 'fact' and no one ever questioned its authenticity."

Well aware of her father's spelling deficiency, Charlotta laughed, "They were either too dumb to catch it or too polite to contradict you."

Then, for the first time, she mentioned his gift of $200,000 to the University of Idaho. He had been waiting for her reaction.

"You made a remarkable and generous gesture last night," Charlotta said. "The spontaneity of your presentation was wonderfully dramatic. I'll bet they'll be talking about it for a long time. I loved the look on President Zimmerman's face when she saw the amount of the check. Incidentally, if you've got another $200,000 you don't know what to do with, you can buy me a two-engine Cessna 421. Just think, we could fly anywhere. No more uncomfortable flights on crummy feeder planes. I could take you anywhere you'd like to go."

Charlemagne was shocked by the magnitude of her request. He had always given her anything she wanted but that was all "peanuts" compared to this! They were nearing Coeur d'Alene and he had to direct her to the Interstate which gave him a little time to think.

"Yes, that's a good idea. You'll have to help me pick it out. First, I think you should find a nice guy, get married and raise a family. I sure would like some grandkids."

Charlemagne really wasn't prepared for the explosion that followed. Charlotta was furious with him and took him to task. "What the hell are you suggesting, Dad, that I go out and marry some guy so you can have some grandkids? Is that the kind of life you want for me? I suppose you think I should go back and live on the reservation and join up with some of those poor girls who don't even know who their kid's father is — just so you can have grandchildren?"

"No thanks," Charlotta continued, "I've got a good job and a career waiting for me in Wichita and I'm not about to blow it to please anybody — and certainly not to get you to buy me an airplane!"

Charlemagne did what he always did when he was admonished by a woman — he kept his mouth shut.

In spite of his pride, his touchiness, his self-centeredness and his ego, Charlemagne had never forgotten the Church of his birth. Now, in his old age, he seldom missed Mass and regularly indulged in gut-level prayer. The religious indoctrination of his youth had been the source of his strength when seeking social justice for Native Americans. Sometimes he simply prayed because there was nothing else he could do.

Charlotta's outburst had cut him deeply but he knew his child and from whence she had inherited her nature. Now, there was nothing else he could do so he silently prayed, "Oh, Lord, I dearly love this beautiful, intelligent half-Sioux daughter. Please keep her and protect her from all evil. Let her heart and soul be cleansed of the sins and transgressions of her White heritage, especially mine and those of the Ferry Boat Captain, Cleopatra. Amen!"

For several miles, Charlotta drove in silence. They crossed the state line into Washington just west of Post Falls before she finally spoke.

Charlemagne was sure it was the power of prayer that had brought her out of her sulk. "I'm sorry, Dad," she said, "but you don't know the abusive treatment I have received all these years on the reservation because I was your daughter and a half-breed. Even my uncle, Painted Horse, called me an Apple — red on the outside and white on the inside. I'm never going back and I will not have children and perpetuate the same cruel hurt on them."

Charlemagne was touched.

"Charlotta, I'm very sorry. I always thought you were happy at Standing Rock. Had I known this was not so, I might have been able to do something about it. I must confess that I was too blind and too self-indulgent to become seriously concerned with your problems."

"Besides," Charlemagne continued, "your great-grandmother and the Lakota Tribe were granted complete custody of you. You know how much I lamented being the unwanted, unloved child of a defaulted mother and a father I have never seen."

After a few minutes, Charlemagne said, "Apparently we both have deep scars from our youth. I guess you're a 'Red Apple' and I'm still the 'Squeak from the Golden Gate' — hey, slow down, we get off at the next exit!"

In her mind, Charlotta could hear her great-grandmother, Loretta Redfeather, telling her, "Sioux people don't cry in front of Whites." Fighting back her tears, she followed the signs to the Spokane Airport.

"Oh, Dad," she said, "it's so sad but funny, too, when you put it that way. I think I'd rather be an 'Apple' than a 'Squeak'. At least I have a loving — and rich! — Daddy."

If I could tell it as it really was! But I can only make fiction of it and write down how it seemed to me that it must have been. So any tale is a shadow of real life, and what we write — an echo of a sound made far away.

Carol Ryrie Brink

PROLOGUE:
A VISIT TO DÜREN

In the old village of Düren, a few miles inside the German border east of Belgium, in the churchyard of St. Hubert's Catholic Church, is a cemetery containing the bones of hundreds of generations of Düren villagers. It is a graveless cemetery with no tombstones and no monuments to identify the names of the deceased or the date of their demise, no prose quotations or verses of love and affection chiseled into stone for a departed wife, husband, mother, father, or infant child. The green turf, the shimmer of sunlight through the full foliage of the Linden trees, the bees hustling for nectar in the flower beds, and the creeping ivy clinging to the old stone wall furnish no clues to the calamity that befell this consecrated ground.

The old American shaded his eyes with his hand. They were sensitive to bright sunlight and he blamed this on his recent operation to remove his cataracts. The truth was he was nearing 80 years of age and without the corrective surgery he would be nearly blind. But it was no fault of his vision that he could not find a tombstone or grave marker in St. Hubert's churchyard.

He was traveling with his son and daughter-in-law on what had been until now a pleasurable and interesting journey. His son had made all the plans and arrangements for the European trip and had driven them in a rented automobile from Austria to this place. They had kept mainly to the back roads and had

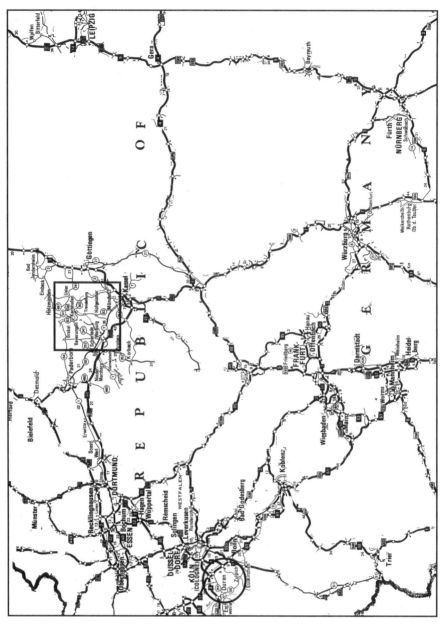

A map of a portion of central Germany. Düren is circled at the western edge of the map. The area around the town of Herstelle is indicated by the box, and is enlarged in the map on page 79. Nüremberg is to the south, near the bottom of the map.

found good accommodations at reasonable rates in small village inns along the way. The three travelers had arrived in Düren the previous night and were staying at the Hotel Germania, Josep Sachregel Str. 20. The village held a significant and troubling place in the mind and memory of the old American.

Düren was the birthplace of his father who, at the age of seventeen, had left his homeland for a new life in America. With the help of the hotel clerk who spoke English, the old American had searched the local telephone directory for names and addresses of living near-members of his father's family.

He was saddened and disappointed when, after intensive inquiries, he found only a distant cousin — a poor, lonely widow dying of cancer in the Düren Hospital. In halting English mixed with German, she told them, "They are all gone. *Alles kaput — alles tot* — Kleins no more."

Fortunately, the widow's English was good enough to give the Americans directions to the parish church where she said they might be able to find some family records. They located the place on a map and, fifteen minutes later, were at the church. They found Father Wolfgang Schmidt, pastor of St. Hubert's, in the parsonage garden.

Father Schmidt spoke only German but he beckoned to some young boys playing in the nearby school yard to join him. One of the boys, about twelve years old, greeted them in English and offered to translate. In this way, the old American heard the story of the graveless cemetery with no tombstones marking the names of the villagers, his forebears among them, who rested there.

Through the young interpreter, Father Schmidt explained, "In World War II, tons of bombs dropped from U.S. Air Force Liberators scored direct hits on the St. Hubert's graveyard and parsonage. The church received only minor damage but the parsonage, containing centuries of church records, was completely destroyed. I believe the remains of your grandparents, aunts, uncles, cousins along with hundreds of ancestors and other Düreners were blown to *schlagen*."

The young interpreter had difficulty finding an English translation for the German word. With dictionary in hand, the old

American's son quickly found the English equivalent, "smithereens." It was not in the young interpreter's vocabulary and he was so pleased to learn such a phonically-tasty new word that he repeated it slowly and loudly several times with a German accent. "Schmit-r-eens, Schmitreens."

Father Schmidt, not understanding the problem, had continued talking and the young translator had to ask him to repeat part of his discourse.

The priest spoke slowly; the young translator occasionally groped for the right word but he seldom needed to refer to the dictionary. "In the dark, tragic days after World War II, Germany's first priority was to provide for the living," said Father Schmidt. "There was not time to dwell on the dead. The ravaged and broken tombstones were confiscated by the authorities for building material, for foundations and such, in the reconstruction of Germany. The scattered skeletons, bones, or anything that could be recognized as remains of the dead were gathered from the bomb craters and the surrounding area and placed in a vault."

"The vault, you see it over there under the tree." The priest pointed to a concrete box four feet wide, four feet deep, and 25 feet long. The inscription on the side read: *"In Erinnerrung and die tulen,"* (In Memory of the Dead). It was apparent that the story of the bombed-out graveyard was not common knowledge to the several young Germans present who listened to the tale with great interest.

As the priest continued telling his story, the three Americans sometimes had to strain to catch the young translator's words. His voice was frequently drowned out by the noise of hammering and the loud conversation of the workers on the other side of the wall. Whenever the noise became too loud, the priest would pause until it stopped. He explained that the parish was building a new kindergarten next to the churchyard; the old burial ground would become a playground for children.

"Very appropriate," the old American told the priest. "I'm sure the spirits of the dead will have no objection." He immediately regretted his words. As if the project depended on the approval or blessing of an old American veteran of World War II.

As a United States combat infantryman with the "Big Red" First Division, had he not been a mortal enemy of his own forebears? Had he not fought only 40 kilometers from here during the bloody siege of Aachen and on to Köln and the Rhine River? Fifty years ago, as an American soldier, he had had no remorse for the havoc wrought on German life or land, no sympathy for the German nation or brotherly love for his German relatives. Fifty years ago, he had refused to acknowledge any ties to these people living in this little German village. Now, it was too late — those to whom he was tied by blood were all gone.

He had never claimed to be a great warrior. Mostly, in combat, he was half-paralyzed with fear. The only times he displayed real courage came when he was mellowed out from drinking the hi-octane French Calvados he carried in his extra canteen. He claimed it was the mix of the alcohol reacting to the alloy of the canteen that gave him relief from his anxieties.

He said nothing about all this to Father Schmidt or to any German but he wondered if they would still be friendly if they knew. Maybe 50 years had erased the memories for them. He wished it had been so for him.

Father Schmidt invited the American visitors into the church. St. Hubert's was undergoing a complete renovation of the interior and access was limited. The exterior of the church was a solid, no-frills structure with thick brick walls. "No wonder it was one of the few buildings that withstood the bombs and artillery fire," the Americans agreed.

After bidding *"auf Wiedersehen"* to the priest and young Germans, they walked across the graveyard to the "no-name-tomb." As they paused at the place where the remains of his ancestors and family members had finally come to rest the old American said, "You know, I have been an enemy and an alien to these people of my blood but I sure am troubled by the desecration that has despoiled this cemetery and the graves of my ancestors."

He continued, "This reminds me of when the Shoshone-Bannock Indian Tribes in Idaho declared war on a bunch of de-

59

velopers who were about to build a housing subdivision on their ancestral burial grounds on a butte overlooking the Boise River." He paused for a moment and then added, "Why are we living humans so sensitive to the disposition of our dead? Must be an inherent characteristic of the entire human race."

The father turned to his son and said, "I guess you were too young to remember when Mrs. Braybrook had the whole town of Grangeville up in arms because the good woman suspected that two graves in China Hill Park were to be opened and the remains moved to Prairie View Cemetery?"

Without waiting for a reply, the old man continued, "Then, there is the unrelenting effort to recover the remains of our missing military in Vietnam. Yes, and I recall the outrage of Okinawa's natives when a few of our rowdy military pillaged and desecrated the sacred urns containing the bones of the islanders' dead. No one is lower than a grave robber, whatever their purpose might be. They were dastardly villains even in early literature and they always will be."

The old American took a last look at the "no name-tomb." His son and daughter-in-law, sensing the old man's mood, remained silent. They didn't understand why he seemed to feel so much personal responsibility for this small graveyard in Düren, Germany. Later, they agreed that "Dad was a little overboard on the graveyard stuff."

They might have been more understanding had the old American told them that he had been here when this place was a living and dying hell — fifty years ago.

MEIN HERR

My father, Matthew Klein, was born in the 1878 in Düren, Germany, and emigrated to San Francisco, California, when he was seventeen. His widowed mother, eager to keep him out of the German military, arranged for him to join her brother, Henry Eschweiler, who was already settled in the city by the Golden Gate.

Truly, it was a new world for Matthew. Separated from his mother and boyhood friends, he was often lonely and homesick for his native village. His entire life in a strange new country was directed by his authoritative uncle. The maxim, *"Nicht kommen rouse auf der Deutsche Haus"* (loosely translated as: "No wild behavior in the German's household.") was the law in the Eschweiler home.

Under his uncle's tutelage, young Matthew learned to speak and read English. A man of many skills, Henry Eschweiler was a self-taught architect, carpenter, musician and inventor. His ingenuity paid off and for many years he received royalties for his design of a machine capable of sewing strips of carpeting together in the manufacture of rugs. As a member of the San Francisco Municipal Band, Henry played the French horn on summer Sundays in Golden Gate Park. His principal vocation was as a builder of residential homes. A master craftsman, he taught his young nephew the carpentry skills that provided Matthew

Above Left: Passport photo of Matthew Klein, circa 1924.

Above Right: Matthew Klein, father of George, with his widowed mother Maria, his sister and infant brother in Düren, Germany, circa 1887.

Left: Joseph Klein, father of Matthew, after he was conscripted into the German Army, circa 1880.

Top:
Identification card of George M. Klein,
U.S. Infantry, World War II

Lower Left:
Robert E. Klein, brother of George, son of
Matthew, U.S. Coast Guard

Lower Right:
Captain George M. Klein, 1942.

Henry Eschweiler, uncle of Matthew Klein, inventor, musician, entrepreneur, with his wife and family. A man of conservative convictions.

with his life-long occupation as a carpenter and builder.

Matthew never forgot his debt to Henry Eschweiler, the only real father figure he had ever known. Matthew's father, the engineer on a steam locomotive, and his fireman had been killed instantly when their boiler exploded. Matthew was only six years old at the time of this tragedy. Years later, he acknowledged that the discipline and early training administered by his uncle were his salvation.

The great San Francisco Fire and Earthquake of 1906 suddenly changed Matthew's life as it did thousands of other victims of that disaster. Unlike older survivors, Matthew viewed the event as an adventure rather than a catastrophe. He was young, unmarried, an alien, and somewhat detached from the citizens who lost their homes, their fortunes or their loved ones. He foresaw the job opportunities that would be created for all trades, including carpenters, in the rebuilding of San Francisco and the construction of new homes in the Bay Area.

Like many survivors of the Fire and Earthquake, Henry Eschweiler and his family moved across the Bay to Oakland. Young Matthew decided this would be a good time for him to get out from under his uncle's wing. He found board and room with the Nels Johnson family who lived just across the street from the Robrechts, another German family who had survived

Anton ("The King") and Marie Robrecht on their 50th wedding anniversary in 1919.

the Great Fire and Earthquake by moving to Oakland. Anton and Marie Theresa Robrecht had eight grown children who fondly referred to them as "the King and Queen" because of their old world customs and Anton's autocratic manner.

Anton had immigrated to San Francisco from Herstelle, Germany, in 1861, sailing from the Baltic Sea in Northern Germany, around Cape Horn at the tip of South America, to the Pacific Ocean and, then, north to San Francisco, a journey of over 12,000 miles and months at sea. He had to be a strong-headed German to endure the hardships of such an undertaking.

After establishing a furniture business in San Francisco, Anton returned to Herstelle. Prior to his departure from his native land, arrangements had been made for him to marry a girl from his village, Marie Theresa Hartman. Several months after the wedding, the newlyweds boarded a ship bound for the Isthmus of Panama. After weeks of sailing, they landed in Central America and embarked on the next leg of their journey.

The young couple proceeded by train across the harsh tropical terrain where they were threatened by bandits, reptiles, malaria, and yellow fever. Completely exhausted, they finally reached the Pacific shore. After weeks of waiting, they found passage on a ship bound for San Francisco. The long sea voyage

Sophie Robrecht and Matthew Klein, George Klein's parents, at the time of their wedding in 1912.

and passage through the equatorial jungle of Central American must have been torture for the 18-year-old Marie Theresa who was pregnant and heavy with child by the time they arrived in the United States. Their son, Anton August, was later the brunt of good-natured teasing by his younger siblings who pronounced him "the Crown Prince, made in Germany."

After moving his family to Oakland, bitter memories of the loss of his home and business in the Great Fire and Earthquake remained vivid in Anton Friedrich Robrecht's mind. He gave little thought to the new young German neighbor, Matthew Klein, who by now was courting his daughter Sophie. I can imagine the exchange between the young Matthew speaking at length in his best High German to tell the old German that he intended to marry his daughter Sophie. Anton probably responded in one word of *"platt deutsch"* (plain German). *"GUT!"*

Sophie and Matt were married in 1912 and I was born exactly nine months later. How lucky for me! I could never have had a better mother if I had made the choice myself. This happy-go-lucky, singing, light-hearted, compassionate, good-natured woman was the antithesis of her father who filled me with awe and apprehension. Grandfather was quite old when I was born and I was constantly reminded by my parents to be very quiet in my *Grosvater's* house.

When I was five years old, my mother told me *Grosvater* was going to take me with him on his regular weekly journey to San Francisco via Key Route Transit, ferry boat and streetcar.

"Remember, George," she said, "you are not to talk to *Grosvater* or he will never take you with him again."

Silence was the game I had to play for this adventure with old, gray-bearded *Grosvater*, the "King," in his black Prince Albert coat, Wellington boots, string bow tie, bowler hat, cane and large green carpetbag. (My cousin Allen later told me the cane converted to a sword!). Shopping in the San Francisco "free market," *Grosvater* soon filled the empty carpetbag with groceries and other provisions. No one asked why he shopped in San Francisco rather than Oakland. They must have sensed that the shopping ritual was an act of repatriation; the old man's heart and memories would remain forever in the City across the Bay.

I have wondered how my grandparents supported themselves considering they had lost everything in the Fire and Earthquake and Social Security was non-existent in the early 1900s. Recently, my older cousin Eleanor told me our grandfather was insured by one of the few companies that paid its policy holders in full for their losses in the disaster.

The traumatic effects of the 1906 Fire and Earthquake were not easily overcome by the victims, including my mother. She frequently drilled her children to stand under the doorjamb at the mere hint of a 'quake. But she did not dwell on the death and destruction. The tales she told and the songs she sang of her happy childhood in brawny "Frisco" were fascinating entertainment to her children. A devout Roman Catholic, she was a good person with a great sense of humor. Raised with five brothers, she became well-versed in the street language of the lusty Barbary Coast and the risqué nonsense of the local burlesque shows.

My father once said, "It never occurs to your mother that there is anything off-color in her tomfoolery." Fortunately, she was oblivious to ridicule and the "Ditties Our Mother Taught Us" did not contribute to the delinquency of her minor children as was predicted by her sister-in-law. Some of the classics from her repertoire were:

DONDERBECK

There was a little German man
His name was Donderbeck
He liked to eat his sausages
With Sauerkraut un Speck.
He had the nicest little store
That ever could be found
His customers they came
From many miles around.

<u>Chorus</u>
Oh, Mr. Donderbeck
How could you be so mean
For to invent such a terrible machine.
The long tail rats and pussycats
Are nowhere to be seen
Since Mr. Donderbeck
Invented his machine

One day a little German boy
Came walking in the store.
He ordered up a headcheese
That came waltzing up the floor.
And while he stood there
He whistled up a tune.
The sausages jumped from the shelf
And danced around the room.

One night the machine went out of order
The wheels they wouldn't go
So Donderbeck he got inside
To see what made it so.
His wife she had a nightmare
While walking in her sleep
She gave the crank a terrible yank
And Donderbeck was meat.

And others:

> *"Hang Jefferson Davis to the sour apple tree*
> *Let him eat the apples 'til he gets the diaree."*

> *"If you know any ladies*
> *That want any babies*
> *Just send them around to me*
> *You lift up the lid and*
> *Out pops the kid with*
> *Half-a-pound of tea."*

> *"Market Street was Market Street*
> *When Filmore was a pup*
> *And Market Street will be Market Street*
> *When Filmore's broken up."*

> *"I'm Captain Jenks of the Horse Marines*
> *I feed my horse on pork and beans*
> *And often live beyond my means*
> *I'm a Captain in the Army."*

These were only a few of her favorites. If she forgot the tune or the verse, she improvised one or both.

Sometimes my father would sing German nursery songs to my baby sister and brother but most of the time he was in no mood for frivolity. He worked 10 hours a day, six days a week, for several different building contractors, one of whom he referred to as "One-nail" McGregor because he skimped on material and wages.

Taking orders from a bully boss was not easy for Matthew. Often he was called Heinie, Fritz, Hun or Kraut because of his guttural German accent. This was the period from 1913 to 1920 when World War I anti-German feelings were vicious and irrational. The thin-skinned, quick-tempered German carpenter hated the provocation and resolved to work to become his own boss. He remembered his uncle's sage advice: "If you're worth $2.00 an hour working for a boss, you are worth twice that much working for yourself."

Gradually Matthew saved enough money to buy a lot and start building a home that he expected to sell for a profit. He worked single-handedly from laying the foundation to shingling the roof. Except for the wiring, plumbing, concrete, and plaster, he did all the construction work unassisted.

Characteristically, he sought no advice or counsel, not even from his uncle, but his mule-headedness got him into trouble. Because of his inexperience, he bought property with a faulty title. A crooked plastering contractor talked him into payment in advance, then skipped without completing the job. Matthew eventually sold the house at a loss. Broke and embittered, he went back to work for wages but not without resolving to try again.

Saving for another start was not easy for Matthew. His mother in Germany was suffering extreme hardship following the collapse of the German economy. The German Mark was worthless and food was scarce in the occupied zone. Matthew was sending her money every month but he was hard-pressed to make ends meet. Trade unions were non-existent and wages were low. Little was left from his paycheck after living costs were paid. Reluctantly, he asked his uncle to finance another home-building venture.

Henry Eschweiler lived up to his nephew's expectations, sparing few caustic words in admonishing Matt for not consulting him on his previous failed house building enterprise. Finally, his uncle agreed to lend him the money — with strings. Most obnoxious to Matthew were the oversight conditions. His uncle was to approve every transaction before execution and no work could proceed until Henry Eschweiler gave his okay. As harsh and detestable as the terms were to Matthew, the house was built and he sold it for a profit.

Typically, Matthew said he could have made it without his uncle's help, not admitting that he had finally learned there was more to the building business than sawing boards and pounding nails. But the venture was worth the pain. Never again did Matthew have to work for wages. On speculation, he would buy a lot, build a modest family home, and usually have it sold within five months from the day he started.

He searched out inexpensive hillside or irregular lots, avoiding expensive excavation by adapting his structures to fit the contour of the earth. Matthew's two- and three-bedroom homes were built according to his personally designed plans and blueprints. They could always be identified by their exposed gables in what was known as the Tudor style, Matt's concept of early European home architecture.

Matthew's disposition depended on the progress of his construction work or the success of the sale. In those days, there were no government housing programs. During a period of depressed housing markets he temporarily moved his family from their rented flat to an unsold home to reduce expenses. He did not handle stress well but Sophie was good at calming him down with humor or making light of his anxieties.

Letters from his mother in Germany telling of hardship and her failing health, added to Matthew's depression. Encouraged by Sophie, he decided to visit his homeland. Before he could make the trip, though, he had to obtain his United States citizenship. I remember the thick, blue hardback American Government book he studied for his night school naturalization classes. With my mother's coaching, he memorized most of the contents of the textbook and easily passed the requirements for citizenship.

Although he needed the citizenship status to protect him from being detained by the German government as a German national, my father was extremely proud to be a United States Citizen.

Years later, he told of his journey by train to New York and steamship to Europe and how difficult it was to reunite with his German relatives. Conversations with them always centered on the hardships they had endured during the war and the French occupation. He felt they resented him because, they implied, he was "living like a king in a rich land while they suffered hunger and oppression." His brother had been held as a prisoner of war by the Russians for three years. When he returned home he found that his wife had given birth to a child that was not his. Bitter and vengeful, he joined the local guerrillas whose mission was to murder the hated black Senegalese occupation troops. The Allies had deployed soldiers from French West Africa to occupy and govern the Rhineland. The Germans considered this to be the ultimate provocation — never to be forgotten!

Matthew's long-anticipated visit to his native village had its unpleasant aspects. Not only did his relatives accuse him of not sending them enough food and money, but his mother began urging him to take his obstinate brother, who was constantly in trouble with civil authorities, to the United States. Luckily, the brother was not in favor of the plan.

There were, however, delightful encounters and events such as a party in his honor organized by his sister and nightly meetings with old friends at the neighborhood beer garden. His most gratifying experience was being identified as an *American Tourist* by a German shopkeeper! I remember my father recounting the incident to my American-born uncles who, because of Matt's heavy accent, found it hard to swallow. But they dared not question the word of "the German!" I know they enjoyed mimicking Matthew's manner of speaking when they were sure he was not about.

Even as a young boy, I sensed the trip to Germany had softened my father's disposition. On Saturdays and during the summer, he took me to the job and tried to teach me how to use tools. An awkward 10-year-old, I never learned to saw a board on the line, hold the hammer by the end of the handle, or drive a nail into the wood without bending it. Whatever job he gave me, I tried to do but I could not meet his standards. Sometimes I followed his instruction but the truth is that I did not have the patience to learn nor did he have the patience to teach me.

Did I have an aptitude for carpentry? Matt said I was a *"dummkopf"* but I built a speeding roller coaster that raced down from the housetop and around the perimeter of the backyard. Charging one cent per ride, I was on the way to great wealth until the heavy foot traffic broke a hole in the roof.

As a "high tech" project, I built an airplane with a 14-foot fuselage and a 20-foot wing span in our basement. Since my father would not excavate the basement wall to let me move it

Left to Right: Robert E. Klein, Lucille Marie Klein Jones, and George M. Klein, children of Sophie and Matthew Klein.

out, the plane may still be in the cellar of 5962 Canning Street, a captive relic of my childhood — ready to soar into the sky on its one-cylinder washing-machine engine fulfilling my dream of emulating "The Lone Eagle," as Charles "Lucky Lindy" Lindbergh also was known.

My father had no enthusiasm for my building projects but he never objected to my careless use of his carpenter tools. I overheard him tell my mother, "I'm surprised by the things that boy can build out of old junk."

My brother Bob, who is twelve years my junior, became a very good carpenter under my father's guidance. He never said it was easy but he did have an aptitude for building and eventually specialized in commercial and public structures in the Vallejo, California, area. I think my sister Lucille was smarter than either Bob or me. She could spell, play the piano, and got excellent grades in school. She was precious to all of us and very special to my father partly because she resembled his mother.

A few years ago, a young friend was mourning the untimely death of his father. He said, "I'm devastated. My father was my mentor, my companion, my confidant, my friend. Now, he is gone and I feel an inconsolable loss and constant sorrow."

I told him, "Ron, I was twice your age when my father passed away. He was eighty. Hardly a day goes by that I am not reminded of him and yesterday, I saw him again in my mirror."

THE GLORIOUS LAND

Marie Theresa Hartman Robrecht, my wonderful grand-mother, was born in Herstelle a. d. Weser, Germany, in 1849. She married at the age of 19 and left her native village for the United States with her husband, my grandfather, Anton Freidrich Robrecht, just three weeks after their marriage.

Bound for the California Gold Rush City of San Francisco, they sailed to Colon, Panama, Central America. Upon arrival, they disembarked and boarded a train that would carry them across the Isthmus of Panama on the new railroad just completed by the USA. By the time the crowded train reached Panama City and the Pacific Ocean, Grandmother was experiencing some discomfort from her pregnancy. Then, it was a miserable eleven-day wait in primitive quarters with the constant harassment of millions of mosquitoes and a variety of crawling and flying creatures before the young couple were able to embark on a sailing ship that would take them to San Fran-cisco.

The seal of the German town of Herstelle.

Grandmother Robrecht's memories of the hardships and the monotony of the journey may be one reason why she never planned a return trip to her beloved Herstelle. More likely, her love for her husband and the eight children she bore in the new land kept her there. Although she would never see it again, Herstelle lived forever in Marie Theresa's heart. Through pictures, words and songs, she passed on to her children and to her grandchildren a love and longing for her native village.

As a child and as a grown man, I often thought of Herstelle as the wonderful, lovely distant village Grandmother had described to me, a magic place where time stood still and all would be exactly as it had been when Grandmother left it many years ago. Perhaps she would be there to greet me on the path as I approached the great castle on the hill overlooking Herstelle and the Weser River.

Pure sentimentality, I told myself, but the vision persisted. That is why, 70 years after Grandmother's death, I made the belated journey to Herstelle, Beverungen, Germany. Never did I doubt Grandmother's description of the village on the River Weser but I knew that time and two devastating wars surely could have been catastrophic for Herstelle. I was prepared for almost anything and I could hardly believe it when I found Grandmother's village almost exactly as she had described it to me many years ago.

A charming antique place, resting on the banks of the Weser, a river that miles away emptied into the North Sea. A system of locks and dikes makes it possible for medium-sized ferry boats and barges to navigate its waters. The long river front of the village presented a neat carpet of grass and shade trees. Viewed from the river, the homes, shops, church, and priory rose in stair steps to the old castle standing high above the village, its solid stone walls punctuated by narrow openings from which defenders could shoot their arrows or other missiles at enemies below.

There it was — Herstelle — just as illustrated on the old picture postcard on Grandmother's dresser that had delighted me as a child. Yes, it *is* the enchanted land of fantasy, close to the home of the famous brothers Grimm whose fairy tales of Snow

White and the Seven Dwarfs, Rumpelstiltskin, the Goose Girl, and many more have become known worldwide as "Grimm's Fairy Tales."

Grimm's legends and children's stories are celebrated in the region today with pageants, parades, and plays. Here also is the cradle of German Mythology with its ancient religious tradition and superstitions. Long ago, Grandmother warned me in a whisper, "Ghosts of the ancient ones are said to dwell deep in the shadows of the forest thickets. We must beware!"

It is only a few blocks from the river to St. Bartholomäus Catholic Church where Grandmother was baptized, confirmed and married. The friendly parish priest, who spoke no English, finally understood our poor German coupled with sign language and located the great old church ledger that contained the record of births, marriages, and deaths of hundreds of generations of Herstelle's parishioners.

Left to Right: Douglas, Father Michael Apostle, and George Klein in the churchyard of St. Bartholomäus Catholic Church, Herstelle, Germany.

HERSTELLE a. d. Weser

Above: Grandmother Marie Theresa Robrecht cherished this very old (possibly 100 years) postcard that kept alive her memories of Herstelle a.d. Weser.

Lower Left: Marie Theresa Robrecht (circa 1926), native of Herstelle a.d. Weser, a place she never forgot. Lower Right: Anton Robrecht, known to family members as "The King," in San Francisco, circa 1875.

A modern-day street scene from Herstelle, Germany.

Top (inset):
St. Bartholomäus Catholic Church in Herstelle, where Anton Robrecht and Marie Theresa Hartman were married in 1869.

Right: Map shows the location of the town of Herstelle in central Germany. The area of this map is indicated by the box on the larger map on page 56.

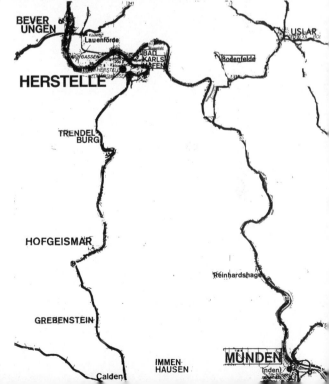

Father Apostle apologized because the records only went back to 1463. It was in that year that enemies had burned the old church to the ground destroying all documents and religious objects. The present church, completed in 1467 on the same site, is still referred to as the "new church."

Almost instantly Father Apostle opened the book to July 6, 1869. It was carefully penned in German script that very loosely translated said:

"7-6-1869 Freidrich Anton Robrecht, age 29, Furniture Handler, San Francisco, California, United States of America, is joined in the sacrament of Holy Matrimony this date to Marie Theresa Hartman, age 19, a maiden, of Beverungen, Herstelle, Germany."

Freidrich, born and raised in Herstelle had migrated to California at the age of twenty. After establishing a successful business in San Francisco he returned to marry Marie Theresa and take her to the home he had made for them in the new land.

I envision Marie Theresa as a young simple woman who loved her family and childhood friends, and who had a deep and religious affection for her home and this village. How hard it must have been for her to agree to leave and travel thousands of miles with no expectation of ever returning.

I'm reminded of a few lines from the play "Fiddler on the Roof":

> "Once I was happy content to be
> As I was, where I was,
> Close to the people who
> Are close to me.
> Here in the home I love.
> Oh, what a melancholy choice this is
> wanting home, wanting him,
> closing my heart to every hope but his
> Leaving the home I love."

Marie Theresa's marriage had been arranged for her between her parents and the Robrechts.

She had been deeply offended when her stepfather reminded her that she was nearing the critical age of twenty and had yet to find an acceptable suitor in Herstelle but the customs and culture of the time dictated obedience to parental decisions.

"It's best for you, Marie," her parents told her. "He's a rich American and will make a fine husband."

True, Marie Theresa had no other prospects for marriage in the village where half of the eligible males had either migrated to America or were inducted into the Germany Army, from which few ever returned. She certainly did not want to become a spinster.

It was not as though she was marrying a complete stranger — the Robrechts were an old and respected family. They could trace their ancestry back for more than 300 years in Herstelle. The name is said to have derived from two words, *Robbe* (seal) and *Recht* (right) — Sealright. This is according to our distant relative Fritz Robrecht, one of many Robrechts living in Herstelle today. The present *Bürgermeister* (Mayor) is Freidrich Robrecht. Grandmother's maiden name, Hartman, is listed many times in the regional telephone directory.

Arranged marriages were very normal at the time and either party could be at risk. That was not the case with this marriage; Marie and Freidrich Robrecht were devoted partners throughout their lives and I have no doubt that their arranged union, which took place at the altar of the very church in Herstelle where 121 years later their American-born grandson would attend Mass, was made in heaven.

Four-and-a-half-feet tall, Father Apostle was almost hidden as he advanced to the altar from the sacristy accompanied by four six-foot-plus altar boys. The Mass was celebrated in Latin and the homily was in German, which left me out except to imagine how it must have been at my grandparents' wedding before this altar so many years ago.

Now, it was the 10:00 a.m. Sunday Mass and the pews were mostly empty, only women and children in this large, solid, stone Catholic church. Were it not for the morning sun flowing through the stained-glass windows it would have been a cool, dark, plain interior, very drab compared to the great cathedrals of Aachen and other European cities with their ornate altars, jeweled fixtures, and brightly colored mosaics.

On entering, I had immediately noticed that something new had been added to this 14th Century parish church. There above me, bright and beautiful, was one of five 10-foot by 20-foot stained glass windows that had been made by the modern method of painting and firing the glass in ovens rather than the early process of chemical-colored glass held together with strips of lead. Particularly interesting about the window depicting the Virgin Mary ascending into heaven was the caption "Donated by Henry Kaiser of Oakland, California, 1962."

I remembered something I had heard years ago — Henry Kaiser, the industrial tycoon of Kaiser Aluminum fame, had immigrated to California from Herstelle with my grandfather. They were friends in those early days when they were both struggling to make ends meet. Later, when the Kaisers became prominent, my mother told me of the early relationship that had been lost in time!

Almost every resident of Herstelle has some close or distant relative who lives or has lived in the United States. They may even ask the American visitor, "Do you know my . . . " uncle, or aunt, or cousin, "who lives in . . . " Chicago, St. Louis, etc.? In 1774, George III, King of England, contracted with Frederick the Great, King of Prussia, for German soldiers to help put down colonial uprisings in America. These mercenaries, known as Hessians, were conscripted from Herstelle and other villages along the Weser. Many stayed in America after the War of Independence and to this day, some of their descendants visit Herstelle and the Weser River Valley searching for traces of their roots.

They must be as surprised as I was when I looked across the river and saw a great concrete flue 300-feet high with a slight puff of white smoke rising from its gut. A modern nuclear energy plant just does not fit in this scene. I would rather not know where they put the nuclear waste.

Perhaps I spent too much time in the Beer Garden but I thought I heard someone call out to me from a passing covered wagon pulled by a magnificent team of horses, their shod hoofs clanking on the cobblestone street, *"Du Langebein, Du Langebein."*

We are all — Douglas, Caryl and George Klein — pleased to have found "The Glorious Land," Herstelle.

"You longlegs."

No one but Grandmother called me *"Langebein."* The mind plays funny tricks.

With the sobering realization that no one was calling me, and after finding the huge, ugly nuclear energy plant in Grandmother's beautiful valley, I finally grasped the reality of the 19-year-old Marie Theresa Hartman's situation. She never was forced into marriage and whisked off to a strange, hard land where she forever yearned to return to Herstelle. No, it was quite the other way around. She was rescued from Herstelle, rescued from a land periodically ravaged by war, famine and pestilence.

One has only to visit the cemetery to see the disproportionate number of graves of Herstelle's young men killed in the Franco-German War, World War I and World War II. The remains of many more lie where they fell. The survivors endured depredation, starvation, confiscatory taxation, paralyzing economic depression, and humiliating military defeats.

Grandmother was spared all of this. She lived well in the new land, her loving husband always by her side. None of her eight children were forced into military service. True, she experienced the loss of her home and treasured belongings in the Great San Francisco Fire and Earthquake in 1906, but her entire family escaped without injury. They had ample resources that allowed them to soon settle in a new home on the east side of the Bay.

Even after they were grown, married and with their own families, most of Grandmother's offspring lived within a few blocks of her house. I lived across the road, and my brother and sister and I were in Grandmother's house as much as we were in our own. She was showered with love and affection because she was a giving, warm, cheerful person. She never failed to have goodies and treats for her grandchildren and she told us fascinating stories, mostly of Herstelle.

If we stayed overnight at her house, we got *apfel strudel* and a cup of real coffee for dessert and slept in a big tall bed, sinking deep into the feather mattress with the goosedown comforters making such a cozy nest.

Yes, I loved Grandmother and I am certainly not disappointed with her dear Herstelle. It truly is all that Grandmother described and more — a great place to come *from*.

The Treasure

This is a true story. Although I was born several years after the Great San Francisco Fire and Earthquake, this story was blazed into my memory by my mother, Sophie Robrecht Klein. All the refugees mentioned in this story have passed on now but their descendants continue to hold and appreciate the valuable "Treasure."

G.M.K.

In the days following the Great San Francisco Earthquake of April 18, 1906, a firestorm raged through the city. Driven by a hot wind, the greedy flames, demanding more and more of the doomed city, forced people to flee their homes and businesses with only a few minutes notice, taking with them only what they could wear or carry.

My grandfather, Anton Robrecht, had come to California in the 1860s from his native Germany. He eventually established a retail furniture store and built a home near the corner of Powell and Clay Streets in what is now a part of San Francisco's Chinatown.

While the firestorm raged in other parts of the city, Anton Robrecht attempted to repair the damage to his home and business caused by the earthquake. As the fire continued its relentless march on the city, he continued to hope. Even when it ap-

Photo of the devastation wrought by the Great San Francisco Earthquake and Fire, taken from the top of the Ferry Building looking west, circa April 25, 1906.

proached to only seven blocks away from them, Papa Robrecht told his family, "They will find a way to stop the fire before it reaches us."

Two days later, he was completely devastated when a law enforcement officer handed him an "Evacuation Notice."

"Sorry, sir," the officer said. "All persons must leave this area by 10 a.m. They are ready to dynamite all structures from here to Kearney Street. It's the only chance to stop the fire."

Papa Robrecht protested but he knew it was futile.

"What a disaster," he said. "Yesterday, I had hope — today, nothing. They are preparing to blow up my life."

Left to Right:
Annie Robrecht,
Blanche Bigué
Robrecht, and Sophie
Robrecht, circa 1904.
Photo courtesy of
Lucille Jones.

He glanced at the decree and noticed it was dated April 19, the previous day. "The *schweinhunds*," he mumbled. "They knew yesterday and waited until now to tell us."

Anton turned to his young daughter Sophie, unmarried and living at home, who was helping him with the cleaning. He said, "Hurry, Sophie, we have only three hours to pack what we can carry. Go to your brother's house and help Blanche. I'll have Augie get your stuff as soon as I tell Mama."

Realizing the gravity of the situation, Sophie was frightened. "Oh, Papa," she said, "I want to help Blanche but Augie doesn't know what I need to take."

"Don't argue. Go quick. I've got to empty the safe. Did you notice where I put my gun?"

"No," Sophie was alarmed. "Why do you want your gun?"

"If you must know, I have to put the dog away."

"Shoot old Wienie? What did he do?" cried Sophie.

"*Dummkopf*, we can't take him with us and we can't leave him here. I hate to do it. Sophie, go quick. *Schnell!*"

The impending fate of the family pet completely shattered Sophie. She was grim as she rushed around the corner and up the stairs to her sister-in-law's flat. Anton's eldest son Tony had married Blanche Bigué in the early 1900s and Sophie was very

Refugees fleeing the devastation of the earthquake and fire. Wheelbarrows, carts and a shank's mare carried the homeless and their belongings, flowing out of Lombard Street to the Presidio. (Edward Zelinsky)

fond her sister-in-law. They were about the same age and had been close friends since childhood.

Sophie had been engaged to Blanche's cousin, Paul DuPree, a worker on the Mt. Tamalpais Railroad. Paul was killed in a tragic accident the summer before the earthquake. Blanche had helped Sophie through her heartbreaking loss. Now, Sophie must help Blanche.

Blanche was sitting on the bed crying. Tony had told her of the dynamite. Putting an arm around her sister-in-law, Sophie tried to comfort her.

"I'm sorry, Blanche," she said. "We are better off than a lot of people. At least we have *some* notice. We must get moving. Papa sent me to help you pack. We can only take what we can carry."

Comforted by Sophie's presence, Blanche started to move.

"Oh, Sophie, I'm so scared. They went to help your mother. I don't know what to do. I packed most of our wedding presents. They are on the kitchen table. All my beautiful presents. How awful to leave them. I don't know how we can take them without a dray."

"I think we can only take the good silverware, the best china and your jewelry," said Sophie.

Blanche agreed. She had already wrapped the silverware in a pillowcase. Together, the two young women packed the china, nesting each piece with newspaper in a large suitcase. They were startled when they heard the gunshot.

"What was that?" exclaimed Blanche.

Sophie knew. She was about to say, "Papa shot the dog," but held her tongue. Instead, she said, "Probably the Army guys scaring off the looters."

At that moment Tony called from the bottom of the stairs, "Let's go, up there. This place is loaded with T.N.T. ready to go off!"

Sophie grabbed the tightly tied pillowcase, Blanche clutched the suitcase, and they rushed down the stairs to join the others on the flight from danger.

The refugees traveled in single file, picking their way through the rubble. Papa first, followed by Mama, Marie, Anne, Sophie,

*Wedding photo of Blanche Bigué and Anton Robrecht (the "Crown Prince"),
at San Francisco, circa 1905. Photo courtesy of Lucille Jones.*

Blanche, Tony, George, Augie, and Herman, with Fritz bringing up the rear. They all understood they were to head for the waterfront. Papa, uncommunicative as usual, told them nothing more. But, as always, they obeyed him. Loaded down with precious treasures, keepsakes and souvenirs, the Robrechts were a remarkable sight.

The acrid smoke and floating ash burned their throats and stung their eyes. Sophie's arms ached with the weight of her bundle. She thought of asking for help from her brothers but they were also loaded down. No one was complaining. She must keep up.

As the family plodded through the damaged streets, their slow progress was halted by a looter who tried to snatch Herman's carpetbag. Sophie welcomed the interruption. Looking down Market Street she could see the Ferry Building still miles away. Her arms were numb but she held on until they reached the waterfront where she dropped her burden and propped herself against a piling.

"Come, come," Papa called. "We go to Pier 15. A boat is there to take us across the Bay to Cousin Karl's in San Pablo."

The Robrecht family had barely boarded when they heard the explosions. They tried to determine the location but the heavy smoke shrouded their view. Gazing over the water and back to the shore, they grieved silently, ministering the last rites to their home, a way of life, and the city they all loved.

The dock on the opposite side of the Bay where the Robrecht family disembarked was a dilapidated mooring but it was good to be on land! One of the boat's crewmen, a former resident of San Pablo, had charted an overland course for their journey to the Karl Wilkie farm.

"It's about seven miles that way," directed the crewman.

"Seven miles! That's impossible!" Sophie almost said aloud. Instead, she reluctantly lifted her heavy burden and, step by step, followed the others.

Except for an occasional *"Mein Gott in Himmel!"* from Mama, the Robrecht family, now a family of refugees, walked quietly through the marshes and into the meadow land. Tired and exhausted, they finally reached the Karl Wilkie farmhouse at dusk where they were greeted with open arms. The Wilkies were shocked and saddened to learn the extent of the Robrechts' losses.

Bertha Wilkie prepared a hearty meal and, for the first time in days, the Robrecht family was at peace.

It was now time to take inventory of what material things they had been able to salvage from the calamity.

"What's in your parcel, Sophie?" Papa asked.

"I've got Blanche's silverware," Sophie replied.

Tony reached for the bundle, lifted it and exclaimed, "Gosh, this is heavy."

He carefully unwrapped Sophie's oppressive burden. "Silverware, my foot," he said. "Look here."

One at a time, Tony removed the items from the pillow case and held each of them up for all to see. Three flatirons, one monkey wrench, and two solid lead cuckoo-clock weights! The rest of the clock had been carried to safety by another member of the Robrecht family.

"Oh dear!" Blanche cried. "Sophie, you took the wrong bundle. You left my beautiful silverware on the table!"

Sophie's face turned ashen. Tears filled her eyes. God must be punishing me, she thought, for not trying to save old Wienie.

Then, her mood changed. "Blanche, you should have told me! You wrapped the stuff. Why didn't you mark it? I'll tell you for sure, if I had known, I would have dumped that old junk in the Bay." Sophie's body shook with anger.

Absorbed in her wrath, she did not hear Papa Robrecht's quiet chuckle. Then, suddenly, the room was filled with laughter. The tension lifted and was replaced by good humor. Blanche took Sophie's hand and they embraced, laughing and crying together.

Mama Robrecht was the only one not laughing. Her only comment was a gentle *"Ach, du lieber."*

It had been a very long day for the Robrecht family.

In later years, the cuckoo-clock hung on the wall of Uncle Tony and Tanta Blanche's living room. As a young boy, I loved the clock my mother had helped carry out of the fire and it al-

Douglas Klein, circa 1938, is fascinated by the cuckoo-clock his grandmother, Sophie Robrecht, helped to rescue from the 1906 San Francisco Earthquake and Fire.

ways seemed to me to be a far greater "treasure" than some old knives and forks. Because of my affection for it and for the people in the story, Tanta Blanche, before she died, gave me the old cuckoo-clock. It now has an honored place in the home of my son Douglas in Missoula, Montana.

THE HISTORY OF
THE KLEIN–NELSON FAMILY

by Mary Anne Dohr
Seattle University, 1992

. . . I dedicate this report to my father, George M. Klein . . . and to my mother, Elvera Nelson Klein . . . .

The legacy of the Klein-Nelson family traces the history of three generations. Many of my ancestors were immigrants to the United States. They fled their native countries of Germany and Sweden, often with little money and few possessions but with the common goal of making a better life for themselves in the United States. They shared common values, endured many obstacles and faced adversity to become Americans.

SAN FRANCISCO AND THE GERMAN CONNECTION

San Francisco was the American home for my German ancestors. My great-grandfather, Anton Robrecht, was the first to arrive in 1855. . . . He came to the United States via sailboat, around the Horn of South America. His reason, in addition to the hope of a better life, was to escape military duty in the German Army. Anton established a business in San Francisco. He later returned to his native town of Herstelle, Germany, and married his sweetheart.

Anton and Marie Robrecht returned to San Francisco to begin their new life together. They raised eight children including a daughter Sophie, my (paternal) grandmother.

Matthew Klein's Journey to America

My (paternal) grandfather, Matthew Klein, grew up in Düren, Germany. When he was age six, his father was killed. My aunt, Lucille Jones (Matthew's daughter), remembers Matthew saying that he worked every day, beginning at age seven. Also, George M. Klein (my father) recalls that in Germany it was common for widows to receive no benefits such as social security. Matthew grew up very poor.

At age 17, a self-reliant, independent and ambitious young man, Matthew Klein came to this country in hopes of achieving a dream not possible in the "old country." He needed to earn enough money to support his Mom, brother and sister in Germany. Once in the United States, he worked as a laborer and learned carpentry. Determination and hard work paid off for my grandfather; he became a successful builder of residential houses and graduated to the American middle class.

The big earthquake of 1906 was a major disaster in the history of San Francisco and a setback in the history of the Klein-Robrecht family. The earthquake created a fire and forced the evacuation of the Robrecht family. They relocated from San Francisco to nearby Oakland. Matthew Klein had also been forced to move due to the earthquake. This unplanned catastrophe led to the chance meeting of Sophie and Matthew who ended up living across the street from one another. Ultimately, they fell in love, married, and remained in Oakland where they raised three children.

The oldest, my father, recalls memories of growing up as a child of German ancestry in the United States. He said it was very unpopular to be a "Hun" during and after World War I.

The kids said my great-grandfather (Anton Robrecht) looked like the "Kaiser" (Emperor of Germany). It seemed very funny to the children to make fun of the German accent and actions. They imitated the way he spoke, not intending disrespect.

My Dad's sister Lucille Jones indicated that they did not speak German in the home because of the negative stereotype. She also remembers Matthew being very proud of the fact that he was an American. He held his head very high when, on a return visit to his native Germany, a German gentleman asked Matthew if he was an American.

Religion was paramount during the years my father and his siblings were growing up. They were raised Roman Catholic and as my aunt Lucille Jones recalls, "I thought of myself as Catholic, not as German." They attended church regularly on Sunday and holy days.

My father, retaining the Klein independent spirit, graduated from high school and set out on an adventure. He was the first family member to go to college. Leaving his native state and city life, he went to college in the small, rural community of Moscow, Idaho. There is where he met my mother, Elvera Nelson.

THE IDAHO HOMESTEAD

My (maternal) grandfather, N. A. Nelson, left his native land of Oland, Sweden. Like many people lured by the great migration of the late 1870s, he came to the United States with hopes of greater opportunity and a better life. Arriving via Ellis Island, he diligently worked various jobs doing anything he could do to save money. Eventually, a brother from Sweden joined him and together they decided to exercise homestead rights. They tried futilely to raise crops on a desert that is now Pasco, Washington.

Temporarily giving up on the farming, my grandfather got a job as the manager of the crew building the Northern Pacific Railroad. A work camp for the crew was set up in Moscow, Idaho. This is where my grandfather met my grandmother, Mary Lind.

As recalled by (my aunt) Elsie Nelson, "Father was helping

Above: Elvera Nelson Klein and her daughter, Mary Anne, circa 1969, on a visit to the Nelson farm three miles southeast of Moscow, Idaho, and the house where Elvera was born.

Left: Mary J. Lind, Mary Anne's grandmother, in Sweden just prior to the family's migration to the United States.

Below: Mary Anne's grandfather, Andrew Lind (far right) with his brothers in Sweden in 1868.

Above: A view of the area around the Nelson family farm.

Left: Nels Nelson, born on the island of Oland, Sweden, in 1860, grandfather of Mary Anne Klein Dohr.

men find rooms and one was located at the home of the Linds. They had a teenage daughter, Mary Josephine, who was destined to become our mother."

The Linds were a family who had immigrated to the United States from their native Sweden. They arrived in 1878 when Mary was about 5 years old. They spent about 8 years in Waseca, Minnesota, before heading west to the Territory of Idaho.

In a book (published in 1973) about Mary Lind's years in Minnesota, E. Nelson recalled, "Besides her interest in reading, Mary was required to do her stitching before going out to play. The daily quota set by her mother was one block for a large piece quilt."

Two years after Mary and E. A. Nelson married, they homesteaded on a farm in the hills of the Palouse, about two miles from the town of Moscow, Idaho. Farming was a life of many long hours and hardships. There were years when crops were ruined and money borrowed from relatives allowed them to pay taxes and keep the farm.

My mother, Elvera Nelson, was the youngest of ten children born on the farm. Her memories of farm life were that, "There were always chores to do. The girls helped Mother in the house and the boys helped Dad do the farm chores."

There were no luxuries or modern day conveniences. Since there was no refrigeration, everything was wrapped and stored in the cellar. The experience gained from growing up on a farm and cooking for harvest crews turned the Nelson women into excellent cooks.

My Aunt Elsie transformed her culinary knowledge and expertise into a lifetime career. She owned and managed several restaurants. Her first venture was opening a tea room in Lewiston, Idaho. She states, "I gained a reputation for French pastries and pies, and for my special Rosebud Chocolate Cake."

My mother, Elvera Klein, is renowned for sourdough cooking. Besides publishing a cookbook on the subject, her recipes have received national recognition through publications by author and humorist Pat McManus.

PERSONAL REFLECTIONS

Researching my family history has given me a sense of the importance of one's cultural identity. Recognizing the hardships experienced by my ancestors has given me insight into what they gave up to become Americans.

Foundations of my ancestry remain a part of my life. My father and his sister both recalled the impact of being raised Catholic. The values and traditions of the Catholic Church were rudimentary in my life. I was educated in Catholic schools from grade school through college. Growing up Catholic has certainly impacted how I view the world.

I see many influences, in particular cooking, sewing and needlework, from my mother's side of the family. Like past generations, I learned to sew and cook at an early age. Like my mother and aunt, I pursued a degree in Home Economics.

As a third generation Swedish-German American, I know very few words of these native languages. Like Kleins of past generations, I have an adventurous and independent nature. Although, I have heard many family jokes referring to the nature of being a "Dutchman," I have experienced no oppression.

Like my grandfather, Matthew Klein, I am also very proud to be an American. However, I feel extremely positive about my German ancestry. As a child, I enjoyed listening to a collection of German music and would sing along pretending to know the words. I anticipate the time when I will be able to visit the native land of my ancestors.

Mary Anne Klein Dohr was born on August 10, 1952, at Grangeville, Idaho; she died of cancer on March 24, 1994, at Renton, Washington.

THE OBITUARIES

This story was inspired by conversations I had with Grace Jordan, the author of Home Below Hell's Canyon *and* The Unintentional Senator. *During World War II, Grace worked as a reporter for the* Idaho County Free Press. *After the war, I became friends with Grace and her husband, Len, who operated Jordan Motors in Grangeville. Len was later elected Governor of Idaho and eventually became a United States Senator. Grace told me how deeply she had dreaded writing obituaries of the war dead as part of her reporting job. This fictionalized version of the experiences of an imaginary reporter for a mythical country newspaper somewhere in Idaho during World War II is my tribute to all my fellow veterans and their families.*

G.M.K.

Gertrude Morgan had just returned to her home in Lewiston from Grangeville, some 70 miles to the south. It had been a long day. She had attended the Garden Club meeting with her friend Dorothy Rice and then spent several hours visiting friends.

Before she could even remove her coat, the phone began to ring.

"Oh, God, I hope that's John," she thought.

Len Jordan, rancher, entrepreneur, politician, Governor of Idaho, U.S. Senator, and husband to Grace Jordan, journalist and author of Home Below Hell's Canyon *and* The Unintentional Senator. *Photo courtesy of Boise State University, Albertson Library, Special Collections.*

She picked up the receiver and whispered her sweetest "Hello."

Her heart sank. The caller was not her beloved husband, Lieutenant John Morgan, assigned to the 2nd Infantry Division at Fort Lewis, Washington.

Instead, a gruff voice barked, "Where the hell have you been? I've been trying to reach you all day."

"Who is this?" Gertrude responded with irritation.

"I'm Bull Horn, Editor of the *Pierce Prospector*," the caller announced. "If you are the daughter-in-law of Bill Morgan, I want to talk to you."

"Yes," Gertrude admitted with some apprehension.

"Bill tells me you took journalism at Washington State College. Is that right?" the caller asked.

"Yes. What is your problem?" Gertrude replied.

"You said it," the editor continued. "I've got a problem. My son Nick has been drafted into the Army and I'm damned short of help. Can you write?"

Gertrude took a deep breath before responding. "Of course, I can write," she said. "Are you offering me a job or just looking for a place to express your frustration?"

No reply.

Gertrude wondered if her caller had hung up or — perhaps — was preparing an apology.

"Hello, hello. Are you there?" she queried.

"Yes, I'm here," the editor continued in the same gruff tone. "I don't have time to jaw with you all day. Why don't you get the hell up here and let me see if you can cut the mustard. Don't worry about the pay. If you're as good as Bill Morgan says you are, I'll give you what you're worth."

The gall of this guy! Gertrude thought. Should I say thanks but no thanks? On the other hand, it could be something I'd like to do.

The abrasive voice of Bull Horn came through the telephone again.

"Well, what do you say?"

Dismissing her annoyance, Gertrude said, "O.K., Mr. Horn. I'll come up to Pierce and talk about it, but I'll have to go to the Ration Board and get some emergency gas stamps. My tank is empty and I'm out of stamps."

"Well, get them and be here on Monday. Good-bye."

Gertrude was usually not quick to judge other people but now she muttered to herself — what a jerk!

Seldom did Gertrude Morgan act on impulse, but on Monday, August 5, 1942, she sat facing Bull Horn in the office of the *Pierce Prospector*.

Bull Horn was saying, "Now pay attention, Gertrude. I'm just going to tell you this once. I write the editorials, the ads, and do the proofreading. Mack Burns — back there — works the linotype. He has a drinking problem so stay away from him. Slug Tate — over there — sets the type by hand. My niece, Sandy Parker, handles the books and circulation. You'll do everything else. Get it?"

Gertrude got it and agreed to start at once. She was now a reporter, a *Prospector* staff member.

She worried about how she was going to move her meager possessions from her furnished apartment in Lewiston but friends came to her rescue. In less than a week, she was comfortably resettled in Pierce in a small house next to the newspaper office

Gertrude adjusted to life in the small mountain community, working 10 to 15 hours a day almost every day. Her letters to Captain Morgan were full of descriptions of her working days and included copies of her newspaper stories.

In one letter, she wrote, "Bull is such a tyrant but he is a good teacher. I'm learning things they never taught in college journalism."

The work kept her mind from dwelling on the great carnage taking place throughout the world and the dangers facing her soldier husband — with one exception. It was Gertrude's job to write the obituaries of the servicemen killed in the war.

"I don't think I can do another obituary," she complained to Bull. "The interviews with the families of dead sons and husbands are so painful it tears me up inside."

Bull pretended not to hear her at first. Then, showing some sign of understanding, he said, "You've got to write full obituaries on all service people. I will not cut your copy. We must support the war effort."

Bull continued, "But you don't have to go out to the cemetery for every burial and listen to those Legion guys shooting guns over the graves. God, it even sends cold chills down my spine! I think that's all that's bothering you. Stay out of the cold."

Gertrude agreed. Someone had to write the obituaries.

Publisher and Editor of the Idaho County Free Press, *"Pop" Olmsted (top) and his sons Gene, pressman, and John, reporter, composer, columnist and ad man. Photo courtesy of the* Idaho County Free Press.

Bull's promise not to cut her copy did not extend to all obituaries. One day, when Gertrude handed him a lengthy obituary of a saintly Pierce woman whose community service had been remarkable, he slashed the story unmercifully.

"We can't run this emotional crap about everybody who's unlucky enough to die," he barked. "So don't start it!"

"But, Bull," she protested, "Mrs. Black will have no other memorial. She deserves this recognition!"

Gertrude's pleading fell on deaf ears. Bull would not budge.

It took about a year for Gertrude to discover that Bull did have a soft side. Sometimes he showed her his poems and the tender, loving letters he wrote to his son, Corporal Nick Horn. Bull claimed to be an atheist but he loaned Gertrude his copy of Peter Clement's book, *The Light of the World* — and made sure she returned it.

Finally, it was 1946 and World War II, the war to end all wars, was over.

There was great joy on the day both Major John Morgan and Sergeant Nick Horn came home. Bull Horn hugged and kissed his son and, in the excitement of the occasion, he embraced every member of the *Prospector* staff, including Mack the linotype operator. Mack, smashed as usual, was so muddled by Bull's spontaneous display of affection he forgot to print the *Prospector's* motto, "Montani Semper Liberi" (Mountaineers Are Ever Free) on the newspaper's banner.

Bull didn't scold Mack, though. He said, "What the hell — now it's freedom for the world."

Sandy Parker, in a burst of fervor, turned to Gertrude and yelled, "Them that write 'obits' also serve!"

Gertrude smiled. Sandy's compliment made her feel good for a few minutes — until she remembered the many flag-wrapped coffins carrying their sad burdens that were yet to reach the Pierce graveyard.

High Jinks

The city of Grangeville lies in the lap of a splendid plateau. At her back are majestic mountains and lush evergreen forests. Even before the town itself was established, the site was the home of the first Charity Grange in Idaho. The Grange, also known as the Patrons of Husbandry, built the first building on the present town site. The building was the Grange Hall and it was constructed under the leadership of Hart Spaulding, son of the pioneer Presbyterian minister of Lapwai, Idaho. Appropriately, the town was named Grangeville, honoring the Grangers.

The Hall was converted into a fort and a hospital during the Nez Perce Indian War of 1877 and 1878. It served as a safe refuge from attacks by the Indians until federal troops came to the relief of the settlers. Joined by local volunteers, the troops brought an end to the hostilities in 1879.

During the conflict, the soldiers of the U.S. Second Infantry were bivouacked a few miles south of Grangeville. The encampment was known as Camp Howard, for Brigadier General O. O. Howard, commander of the Department of the Columbia, headquartered at Vancouver, Washington Territory. The General's mission was to force the Indian tribes to stay within the borders of the reservations and to protect the settlers. Denying the Nez Perce people access to their ancestral lands had precipitated the war.

The Grangeville Grange Hall, circa 1900. Built in 1876, it served as a center for Grange business, community events, and, fortified, as a refuge and hospital during the Nez Perce War. Photo courtesy of the Idaho County Centennial Committee.

Most days, the soldiers were on the move, scouting the prairie and river gorges for hostile Indians. The camp at the foot of the mountain was not fortified but did provide a base for command, shelter, recreation and some security. It was located on the present John Schoo place just south of Grangeville at the Fish Creek County Road. Now, the road continues up to the Gospel Hump Wilderness. The old, gold boom town of Florence, now a ghost town, is 42 miles south at an altitude of 6,255 feet. None of the original Camp Howard buildings are standing today although various artifacts with army insignia, crockery, and gear have been found at the site.

The history of the Grangeville area is varied and fascinating. The fossil beds at White Bird, the recently discovered mammoth elephant bones at Tolo Lake, the story of Chief Joseph, the heritage of the Nez Perce, and the lives of the early pioneers and miners are stories that have been or are yet to be told — some factual, some imagined.

On the southern slope of the timbered mountains, about two miles from town, is a small clearing the size of a football field. It

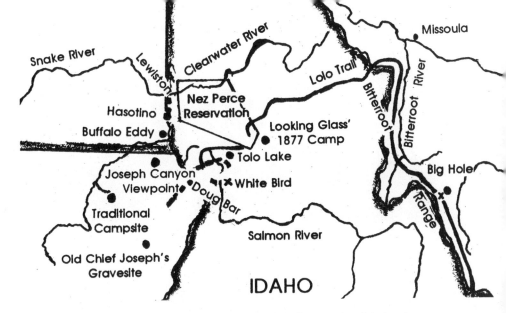

Created in 1965, the Nez Perce National Historical Park comprises 24 sites in Idaho, all significant to the history of the Nez Perce Tribe and the United States. A bronze plaque at the entrance to the park's Spaulding Museum of Nez Perce Culture commemorates the original promoters of the park, of which the author is one.

is the only open, untimbered place on the mountain and is known as "High Camp." The open patch is 1500 feet above the prairie floor and in the line of sight from the window of the office I once occupied on the second floor of the old Flanigan Building. I often speculated on the events that would explain the name "High Camp." Allen Adkison told me it had been an outpost for General Howard's troops in the Indian Wars.

Some years ago Owen Shirley and I tried to drive up to High Camp in an old army jeep. The road, blocked with fallen trees, deep washouts, and steep slopes, was impossible. We had to leave the vehicle and walk what seemed like two country miles to High Camp. We went there to explore the possibility of erecting for the Christmas season a lighted cross that would be visible from Grangeville and perhaps far into the prairie.

It was almost dusk when we finally reached High Camp. Looking north, we could see the lights of town and the shimmering of the setting sun reflecting on the windows of far away prairie farmsteads. We agreed that this was a great site for the cross and the logistics for providing electric power and transporting materials were worked out. Surprisingly, the clearing was much steeper than it appeared from town and the cross, built on the sharp incline and forming a great illuminated crucifix more than 100 feet across, appeared to be suspended in the night sky.

For a few seasons, the cross at High Camp burned bright in the cold December night, visible from Grangeville and far across the Camas Prairie. Unfortunately, the light bulbs made great targets for hooligans with guns. However, the great illuminated cross still shines from High Camp through the Christmas and Easter holidays.

No one has found artifacts or evidence proving that High Camp was an outpost for the Pony Soldiers in the Nez Perce Indians Wars. Tactically, High Camp offered the most strategic observation opportunity of the entire mountain area. It is not unlikely that Captain Doolittle, Commanding Officer of Camp Howard, realizing the vulnerability of the heavy timbered encampment, posted sentinels where they had the best field of visibility. Was that place High Camp?

With field glasses, the soldiers could detect, identify and report hostile Indian movements on the flat terrain below and as far north and west as Tolo Lake. Elta Arnold, historian and former Superintendent of Schools told me, "Without solid proof, relating High Camp to the Indian Wars of 1878 is an illusion."

But how many fragments of historical information are based on infallible evidence? The name Idaho doesn't mean "Light on the Mountains" and George Washington didn't cut down the cherry tree. My enthusiasm for the "army observation post theory" was dampened, however, when Foster Morgan provided the answer:

"That clearing on the mountain south of town was made by woodcutters," he said. "Making cord wood was an important business 70 years ago and they called that place 'High Camp.' The woodcutters had an operation at the foot of the Mountain they just called 'Camp.' The 'High Camp' location was close to thick stands of Western Larch commonly known as Tamarack.

Tamarack was judged the best fuel because it burns hot and long and is easy to split but it does a lot of snapping and crackling while it burns, spitting hot coals out of an open fireplace."

Foster Morgan, a retired rural mail carrier, is a Grangeville native who as a sportsman, philosophical student of local history, and a mail man, has explored most roads, wilderness trails

Left: Chief White Bird, who camped near the site that is now White Bird and for whom the town is named. Photo courtesy of the Idaho County Centennial Committee.

Right: Captain Darius Bullock Randall, killed in action in the Nez Perce Indian War, is buried in the Mt. Idaho Cemetery. His gravestone reads: "D.B. Randall died on July 5, 1877, aged 40 years, 5 months, 22 days." Photo courtesy of the Idaho County Centennial Committee.

Above: The new White Bird Grade (U.S. 95), completed in 1975, shortens the distance between the Salmon River and the summit by more than five miles. It still provides a spectacular view, including an overview of the White Bird Canyon Battlefield of the Nez Perce War of 1877. Below: The old White Bird Grade, built in 1921 by convict labor and steam operated shovels, zig-zagged to the summit, climbing more than 3,000 feet in about 11 miles, and was hailed as a remarkable engineering feat. Photos courtesy of the Idaho Department of Transportation.

ERECTED IN
MEMORY OF THE
SEVENTEEN VOLUNTEERS
WHO ENGAGED IN BATTLE
WITH THE INDIANS
2000 FEET EAST
FROM THIS POINT
WITH TWO KILLED AND
THREE WOUNDED THE
5TH DAY OF JULY 1877
DURING THE NEZ PERCE INDIAN WAR
CAPTAIN D. B. RANDALL,
C. M. DAY, JAMES BUCHANAN, H. C. JOHNSON
F. A. FENN, FRANK D. VANSISE, L. P. WILMOT,
A. D. BARTLEY, CHARLES JOHNSON A. B. LELAND,
E. J. BUNKER, CHARLES W. CASE, B. F. EVANS,
J. L. CEARLEY, WILLIAM B. BEEMER, D. H. HOWSER,
GEORGE RIGGINS.
DONATED AND ERECTED BY EVAN EVANS
THROUGH IDAHO COUNTY PIONEER ASSOCIATION
GRANGEVILLE, IDAHO
THE 5TH DAY OF JULY 1931.

Marker (formerly located one mile south of Cottonwood, Idaho, and now in safe storage) in memory of the seventeen volunteers who engaged in battle with the Nez Perce. Captain D.B. Randall was killed in that skirmish.

and waterways in Idaho County, an area larger than the state of Massachusetts. Foster has great credibility with his peers; he has been everywhere in the county and has talked to a lot of folks along the way! So, reluctantly, I relinquish the "High Camp as a Pony Soldier Observation Post" story.

High Camp will survive as an important landmark to prairie people regardless of whether or not it qualifies as a historical site of note. For years, the clearing has been a reliable weather gauge. It has been customary for folks to watch High Camp for the first blanket of snow, heralding the coming of winter, and the vanishing of snow, signaling the arrival of spring. Many have wagered on the exact dates of these events.

After a hard winter, people enjoy a little diversion. One year, the betting on the arrival and departure of the snow from High Camp became organized. You could make as many wagers on the appearance or disappearance of snow from High Camp as desired for five bucks a crack.

The judge for the contest was the editor of the local newspaper, considered by all to be a fair and honorable man. By coincidence, he was the same person who sold newcomers a ticket for one dollar entitling them to: "Play Kick The Can at the Old Rock Pit East of Town on all Friday the 13ths at 12 Noon (good for life)."

On each Friday the 13th, from a hidden spot near the Old Rock Pit, this gentleman would observe how many suckers had bit on his hook. He did get some unbelievable catches (I bought a ticket but forgot to show) and it tickled him pink — but he never revealed himself.

Grangeville had a surplus of pranksters. Most were Main Street businessmen harassing each other. Gib Eimers had his Real Estate office on Main Street next to the Blue Fox Theater. Every day he went home to lunch but often forgot to lock the office door. One day, he returned from lunch and found his office bare to the walls — no furniture, nothing but the telephone. George Pfeiffer, owner of the Sport Shop, had borrowed Miller's Hardware truck and with the help of Dick Large had cleaned out Gib's office.

There was a good-sized crowd on hand when an astonished, hopping-mad Gib Eimers returned from lunch to discover he had been "robbed." After relishing every minute of Gib's distress, George and Dick returned the furnishings to their rightful place, knowing not what reciprocal act was in store for them.

The many pranks, some ingenious, some crude, seldom resulted in anyone being hurt or suffering serious personal or business loss but the "High Camp Lottery Caper" strained the limit.

At the time of the early snowfall on the mountain, around Thanksgiving Day, Glenn Ailor, mortician, and Bunk Walker, oil distributor, secretly traveled up the mountain to High Camp. There, under the cover of night, they spread two large white sheets on the ground holding them in place with heavy rocks. It was a tedious task. They had to walk part of the way on a slippery trail and work in the dark. Bunk sprained his ankle and Glenn had to carry him back to the pickup.

Bunk and Glenn kept mum on their venture, even to their wives. Their next step was to enter the big predicting game, picking the day and time the snow would completely disappear from High Camp.

Winter passed. Spring arrived. People looked up at the mountain and said, "Ain't that damn snow ever going off High Camp?"

Then one morning in late May, on the exact date and time of their "prediction" for the departure of the snow, Bunk and Glenn pulled the white sheets off the High Camp and returned to town to collect their winnings.

It was too good a joke to keep to themselves and the pranksters confessed the caper to the Lion's Club and donated all of their winnings to the Lion's Eyesight Foundation. There were no hard feelings but that ended the High Camp game of "skillful" weather prediction. The sponsors attempted to replace the intellectual forecast with a simple lottery but interest ran out.

The confession and donation of their winnings to charity saved Glenn and Bunk from any catastrophic "paybacks." That was not the case in the Gib Eimers' office furniture "robbery."

The principal perpetrator of that caper, George Pfeiffer, made a business of trapping rattlesnakes in the rock caves at the foot of Harpster Grade and selling the venom to a pharmaceutical company for medical purposes. He also sold the meat, skin and rattles. As a tourist attraction, George kept several live rattlers in a good-sized glass cage in his sporting goods store. One day, the town was put on alert. Someone had released the snakes from the cage at Pfeiffer's, an obvious payback but only kangaroo justice.

No saga on High Camp can close without recognizing our neighbor Lois Small who went up to High Camp early one morning by herself and shot a nice fat buck deer, dressed it out, returned home, and prepared breakfast for her husband Brownie and the kids.

That *is* High Camp!

MEMORIES OF
GRANGEVILLE AND IDAHO COUNTY
DURING A TIME OF CHANGE

On a gray November day in 1949, Walter McAdams, proprietor of the Mountain View Club, Grangeville, Idaho, shot and killed a man in cold blood. The murder took place on Main Street in front of McAdams' establishment where he then, in full view of witnesses, stood over the dead man holding the smoking gun.

This homicide made a real impression on our entire family, especially since we were "newcomers" to Grangeville having arrived in town just about the time of the killing.

The reason for the murder was not made public. After a quick inquest, McAdams continued to tend bar. He never spent a day in jail. This added to our family's apprehension. "What kind of a place is this?" we asked. "Is this normal? Does anyone here care about law and order?"

Frankly, the incident had such an impact on all of us that we considered returning to Moscow and foregoing our commitment to start a new life and business in Grangeville.

We will always be grateful to our friends and neighbors who assured us we were not in the untamed West and there was no traffic jam on "Boot Hill." We found that some of the finest people on earth lived in Idaho County. The violence remained in our minds but we decided to stay in Grangeville. We never regretted our decision. We loved Idaho County and lived and worked there for almost twenty years.

The period beginning a few years after World War II and extending into the 1960s was a time of transition and adjustment. The pressures of the War Economy were gone. Veterans were home and settled into civilian life; our farmers were still feeding the world; and the national building boom had energized the local timber industry. Some people welcomed the challenges brought about by change, others preferred the status quo, and many didn't give a damn one way or the other. Political and economic issues were plentiful and conflicts inevitable.

Following are a few of our memories of these changing times:

School Daze

Consolidation of School Districts set off a war to the death in the early 1950s. John Asker, Grangeville, and John Hanley, Cottonwood, of the Idaho County School Board took the brunt of the fight for consolidation. Most everyone in the county was involved in the process. To say people were upset is an understatement. There were threats of violence and open boycotts of businesses coupled with intimidation of anyone who expressed an opinion one way or another. Whenever the situation cooled off, the Lewiston Tribune found a way to stir things up by quoting some very derogatory remarks made by some "know-nothings" from either side of the issue. It helped sell their newspaper but it was tough on those level heads from both sides of the County who eventually accomplished a workable compromise for school consolidation.

Unsafe and Tedious

In 1955 the Reader's Digest published a story of the adventures of a family who were faced with the challenge of ascending the White Bird Hill switchbacks with a 40-foot trailer house in tow. Of course, the story was exaggerated and mostly fiction. It did make the White Bird Hill famous, though, especially after Hollywood made a movie from the story entitled "The Long, Long Trailer" starring Lucille Ball and Desi Arnaz.

This, and other events, brought pressure on the State Highway Commission to relocate the White Bird Hill road to a safer and less tedious route. Hearings were held throughout the county to get user input to help the state decide which of several proposals they would select for relocation of this notorious section of Highway 95.

Grangeville leaders said it was vital to the town's welfare to build the road up the Hill and over the summit, skirting the west edge of the city. Cottonwood beat the drums for a route up Graves Creek, bypassing Grangeville by about 12 miles. Everyone in the county got in on the act and the hearings were jammed. Some warned that if the road went over the Hill, it would be closed by snowdrifts three months of every year. Others claimed a road up Graves Creek would be washed out every time it stormed. It was a real talk-a-thon.

Hoping to enlist the support of Lewiston and Moscow for the Graves Creek route, the Cottonwood folks, led by George Kopczynski, arranged a meeting at Moscow. When word of the meeting reached the uninvited Grangeville leaders they quickly arranged to attend. They showed up in force, crashing the gate and disrupting the meetings. Although they were not welcomed by the Cottonwood delegation or the people from Lewiston or Moscow, it was clear that the two larger communities did not want to get involved in a fight between Grangeville and Cottonwood. There were no winners that day.

Several weeks later the Highway Commission announced their decision to build the new road over the top of the Hill and run it along the west limits of Grangeville. It was great news for the leaders in the county seat.

RADIO MAKES WAVES

The Idaho County *Free Press* and its owners, John and Gene Olmsted, exercised considerable influence in Idaho County and they made a few enemies. John said his father, Pop Olmsted, had told him, "You never print anything derogatory about a person unless he lives at least 200 miles from Grangeville or works for the federal government."

The Olmsteds held religiously to the rule. They were not too happy, however, at the prospect of a radio station in Grangeville. Rumors of market surveys and applications for a Grangeville radio permit had been floating around for a couple of years. Finally, a fellow from Spokane showed up one day and reported that he had the approval of the FCC to build a radio station.

Hub Warner had a great radio voice, a flair for the dramatic, and hardly any money, but he did have the credentials to operate a radio station. Cashing in on his charm, Hub was able to obtain enough credit to build "KORT, The Voice of the Camas Prairie."

Oh, how great to hear the local news and community events broadcast from our very own radio station! Hub worked from sunup to sundown at the mike. He was a one-man show. His wife Helen kept the books and Luin Dexter, a local high school boy, was his assistant announcer.

Hub welcomed all public service programs. This was the time for using this great new media for political campaigns and local politicians were eager to have their candidates go "on the air."

Gilbert Eimers, a popular and responsible Grangeville businessman was running for the State Legislature on the Republican ticket. The Idaho County Democratic Committee decided it would be great to have Bill Cosner, a Democrat from Lewis County, make a radio statement on behalf of Gib's opponent. After a disastrous and almost libelous 30-minute tirade against Gib by Bill, the local Democrats hung their heads in shame. They tried to excuse themselves by saying, "We never told him to say that."

Members of both political parties who heard the broadcast were outraged at the attack on Gib. They said, "There was no call for that. He is one of us."

That ended political slander on the radio.

Pop Olmsted's rule for his newspaper proved to be just as appropriate for the airwaves!

After a few years, Hub sold the station to Eb and Kay Brainard, who had moved to Grangeville from Vermont. Eb had been a director for the Kate Smith show of "God Bless America" fame. The Brainards did a good job and served the entire county very well. Of course, Eb had a New England accent that was considered rather amusing to local folks, particularly when he referred to the "Sall-mon Rivah." It cracked them up.

ROCKING CHAIR MONEY

"Rocking Chair Money" (unemployment insurance) kept the local economy going during the winter months throughout the 1950s. The local sawmills shut down for repairs and logging came to a halt. Farm and livestock activity slowed down. People had time to follow the conduct of the state Legislature in session at Boise. Sad but true, most Idaho County citizens had a low opinion of politicians unless they were friends or relatives.

There were no "flaming liberal" elected officials in Idaho County.

Joseph Kashmitter, Democrat, a State Representative from Cottonwood, received statewide notoriety for voting "No" on practically every bill brought before the House. Joe frequently addressed solid Republicans and received warm support from them.

Grangeville's City Attorney, Democrat William J. Dee, when elected State Senator from Idaho County, gained great favor with conservatives for his frugal approach to state budgets. With a few breaks he could have been elected Governor. The same could be said for Jack Tacke, Democrat State Representative from Cottonwood; Tony Wessels, Democrat State Representative from Greencreek; and Nels Solberg, Democrat State Senator from Grangeville.

In the name of fiscal responsibility, Republican Len Jordan from Grangeville closed the Lewiston Normal College when he was Governor. It was called political suicide at the time but Jordan went on to become a United States Senator from Idaho.

When it came to state government, the message from Idaho County voters was loud and clear: No more taxes — no more laws or regulations — don't interfere in our business! It was often quite the opposite when it came to local, county and city governments. People were willing to pay for streets, schools, libraries, community buildings and parks.

BIG GOVERNMENT

Idaho County folks usually tolerated their local elected officials but U.S. Government employees were mostly viewed as "outsiders." In the early 1960s, the Forest Service was directed by Congress to seize all unproved mining claims, hunting camps and squatters' abodes located on all public lands. This and the Fed's decision to enforce the provisions of the Wild and Scenic Rivers Bill on the Middle Fork of the Clearwater River provoked many local people. After years of mildly restrictive use of the Nez Perce National Forest, people resented the new tough restraints placed on the Public Lands.

Strictly regulated timber sales, establishment of wilderness areas, closed Forest Roads, and reduced livestock grazing all were extremely irritating. Nez Perce Forest Supervisor A.W. Blackerby and his predecessor John Milodragovich, both good administrators, reminded people they were only doing their job and asked, "How come no one complains about the dollars the U.S. Forest Service and its employees spend, the full-time and part-time jobs, as well as the thousands of dollars for improved campgrounds, roads and other facilities?"

"Who would dare complain about getting U.S. Dollars from way back in Washington, D. C.?"

"Better than giving it to the United Nations or some country we don't even know," was the local response.

BANK ROBBERS

Speaking of money, some people were devastated when the President of the Cottonwood Bank, W. W. Flint, reported to Sheriff Bud Taylor and the FBI one morning that burglars had broken into the bank during the night and emptied all the safe deposit boxes. It was rumored that the thieves stole thousands of dollars in cash stashed away by some prominent money grubbers. The Internal Revenue Service was interested in getting figures on the victims' exact losses but the question was moot.

Little compassion was expressed for the losers and jokes came from all quarters on where *not* to put your money.

There were only two banks in the whole of Idaho County at the time, the Grangeville Branch of the First Security Bank, managed by Ward Dempsey, and the recently robbed Cottonwood State Bank. In 1958, Bill Ketchum, sawmill owner, and Owen Smith, logger, promoted a new "Central Idaho Bank" in Grangeville. Floyd Swanson became manager and it was affectionately known as the "North Bank of the Salmon River."

All financial institutions experienced rapid growth in the 1950s and the local merchants enjoyed improvements in their sales. There was concern the improved Highway 95 north to Lewiston, including the elimination of the old Winchester Grade, would reduce driving time and result in Idaho County people going to Lewiston to shop. There was an impact for a short while but the improvement of the White Bird Hill and the new Lewis-Clark Highway to Montana brought more traffic to Grangeville and all across the Prairie.

THE ANCESTRAL LANDS

Credit for the promotion and final completion of the Lewis-Clark Highway as well as the establishment of the Nez Perce National Historical Park goes to the Lewiston civic and political leaders — particularly to Bill Johnson, Editor of the Lewiston Tribune. The scenic road, following the beautiful Selway River, bordering the wilderness area, and marking the historic Lewis-Clark expedition through the Bitterroot Mountain Range, was completed in 1962.

For years, Lewiston had planned for the opening of a viable port to the sea. The new Lewis-Clark Highway permitted the trucking of food and fiber from the east to the new Port of Lewiston. It was proclaimed a plus to the economy of the entire county.

The new highway and the proposed Nez Perce Historical Park sparked interest in the history of Idaho. The two volumes of "Pioneer Days in Idaho County" by Sister Alfreda Eisensohn of St. Gertrude's Convent at Cottonwood were "best-sellers" throughout the state. To capitalize on this interest, the Grangeville Border Days Committee decided to dedicate the 1952 Border Days Celebration to the Nez Perce Indians and emphasize the 75th Anniversary of the termination of the Indian war of White Bird Canyon.

A Queen Is Crowned

Roy Stockham, the energetic chairman of the Border Days Committee, soon had the complete cooperation of the Nez Perce Tribe. They agreed to build a village of teepees within the Rodeo Grounds. They also agreed to join in the parade in full regalia for the entire three-day event. Bill Cone, Sr., carried a big purse of silver dollars with which he rewarded Indian families for their colorful participation.

In keeping with the theme, a bona fide Indian girl had to be found to compete in the contest for Border Days Queen. Georgia Mae Ellenwood, a Kooskia High School student and a full-blooded Indian, was the logical choice. Her parents agreed that Georgia Mae could enter the contest.

There were some obstacles; Georgia Mae did not ride a horse, lacked money to buy a suitable rodeo costume, and needed funds to complete dental work that would enhance her good looks. The committee did not hesitate to provide money to resolve all of these problems.

Georgia Mae was a beautiful princess. On July 2 and on July 3, she rode her horse into the rodeo area for the Grand Entry and bowed gracefully before the grandstand. She was marvelous — particularly since she had learned to ride in just a few months on a less-than-spirited mount.

On the glorious Fourth of July, the final day of the event, before a packed grandstand, Georgia Mae Ellenwood fell off her horse! A muffled moan came from the crowd. Georgia Mae stood

Right: Rodeo Queen Georgia Mae Ellenwood, distinguished member of the Nez Perce Tribe, Grangeville, Idaho, 1957.

Below: Nez Perce Tribe members at Border Days Rodeo and celebration, Grangeville, Idaho, 1957. Left to Right: Grandmother of Gene Ellenwood, Justin Parson, Mr. McConville, Al Williams, Richard Ellenwood, Georgia Mae Ellenwood, Gene Ellenwood's mother, and an unknown person. Photo courtesy of Idaho County Centennial Committee.

up, brushed off the dust and dung of the arena, caught her horse, remounted, circled the arena and saluted the grandstand. Suddenly, the silence was broken by a roar of applause from the stand. Georgia Mae won the contest. The honor was bestowed upon her by the Rodeo Committee for poise, courage and great dignity.

WHICH WITCH?

Border Days, the Idaho County Fair, the Salmon River Rodeo, Kooskia Days, the Elk City Celebration, all required long hours of dedicated work by many people. These traditional celebrations not only preserve the historical integrity of the county but help to unify the community.

Nothing can lead to disunity faster than the lack of domestic water. Most Camas Prairie towns experienced a shortage of domestic water in the early fifties. Cottonwood experienced the most critical shortage. When all methods failed to locate water, the city fathers, in desperation, engaged a self-proclaimed "expert geological water-locating engineer" from California.

Mr. Reese became an instant hero — he located a 300-gallon per minute well on his first try for the city of Cottonwood. His fame was great and his services were in demand throughout the Prairie. Unfortunately, he proved to be dead wrong on several sites he had selected. Grangeville drilled several wells on Reese's recommendations. Most were either dry or of low capacity.

Tempers flared when faucets went dry in the warm summer months. Water rationing was mandated but this only aggravated the situation. There was talk of bringing water up from the Clearwater or Salmon Rivers. Every kind of water witch, crackpot and false prophet claimed they could find water. All to no avail. But hope springs eternal. Like gold, water is where you find it and the search continues.

L.I.D.

The Medieval Knights of Arthurian times had the Round Table; Grangeville townsmen had Coffee Breaks. The twice-daily ritual was held at the Stockman's Bar or the Kandy Kitchen. Attendees were inter-changeable. Participants sat at the big booth in the Kandy Kitchen or on the stools at the Stockman's Bar. There were no restraints on topics of conversation. Women seldom joined in, although Cora Devine, the owner of the Stockman's Bar, never hesitated to voice her opinion on any subject that arose.

While there was considerable horse-play, some serious business took place at the Coffee Breaks. Community leaders, including federal, state, county and city elected officials, often joined the "coffee gang." Sometimes a consensus was established on many political and economic questions.

One idea hatched and launched during an unusually productive session was the notion of forming Local Improvement Districts to pave Grangeville streets. After many weeks and a great deal of wrangling, the proposal was presented to the City Council. From then on, it was a matter of grinding out petitions, conducting public hearings, and dealing with legal technicalities.

City Attorney William J. Dee, his successor William B. Taylor, Clerk June Edwards, City Water Superintendent Art Canaan, and Street Supervisor Earl Heath deserve special credit for their performance in clinching the construction of Grangeville's first L.I.D. There were times when the project appeared doomed to fail but by persuasion, tenacity, and gerrymandering, several blocks of Grangeville streets were paved.

Memories linger on — L.I.D. No. 1 wasn't easy but others followed as more and more property owners recognized the value of the paving.

Two unconventional street-building techniques were incorporated in the first project. The Portland Cement Association had been experimenting with a process known as "Soil Cement." This process consisted of roto-tilling the existing graveled streets then spreading cement over the surface and mixing the soil, gravel and water with road graders and tillers. The resulting mix provided a firm, deep road base over which was applied a thick layer of asphalt. To prove the value of the soil cement, test cores were taken at random. The core tests convinced everyone that the decision to apply this soil cement method was a good one.

A matter of great debate was what to do about curbing and gutters? Concrete curbs and gutters would almost double the cost. The engineering firm suggested a new process of building curbs with a machine that extruded asphalt into black barriers.

It was fast and cheap but folks were skeptical.

"The damn things will melt down in hot weather."

"First time you hit them with a car, they'll crumble."

"They look funny."

People soon became accustomed to the black strips, most of which stood the test of time.

Bitter opponents of street improvements said "You're breaking us with this unnecessary expense. We will all end up with grass growing on our empty streets — dead broke!"

That was in 1956, more than forty years ago.

Main Street

Was it a matter of rewarding Grangeville for cooperating in the planning for the new section of Highway 95, White Bird Hill, or a punishment for all the flack? Whatever the reason, the Idaho Highway Department decided to reconstruct Grangeville's Main Street, State Highway 13. Actually, it was high time to improve the battered thoroughfare. The Grangeville Chamber of Commerce had pleaded for years for the State to do something.

When the time came, Owen Shively, Manager of the local office of Washington Water Power Company, accurately described the coming ordeal when he said, "You can't make an omelet without breaking the eggs." For twelve weeks, Main Street resembled a war zone. The dust, noise, bumps, detours and confusion were almost unbearable. Merchants suffered loss of business, damage to property, and threats to their sanity.

Some folks were surprised to learn that a creek ran under Main Street in the vicinity of the old Table Supply Grocery on the south and beneath Miller Hardware on the north side. The channel drains an area south of the city causing heavy flooding during the periods of heavy rain or rapid snow melt. Years ago, a pharmacist was drowned in the basement of his drug store when he was surprised by a flash flood. More recently, the same place, now the basement of Gib and Lloyd Myers' Table Supply, was flooded again, resulting in the loss of hundreds of dollars of inventory.

Dedication of Grangeville's new Main Street, 1962. Left to Right: Mayor George Klein; Postmaster Miles Flanigan; County Surveyor Joseph Montell; Banker Harriman Henry; Wes Jenkins, Manager of Jordan Motor Company; Jerry Walker, jeweler; unknown; Norman Cossley, State Urban Engineer; Phil Marsh, District Highway Engineer; boys in front unknown.

To rectify the flooding situation, a culvert with twice the capacity of the old one was installed.

The disorder and the chaos of the reconstruction project provided "field days" for hundreds of "sidewalk engineers." Few road jobs ever had the inspection, observation, scrutiny, or examination this project received from the local citizenry. Kibitzing was mostly good humored but some complained the job took too long.

Upon completion of the reconstruction, there was grumbling from some about having to park parallel to the curb rather than at an angle, but most citizens admired the smooth black surface and the clean white traffic lines. People felt so good about the opening of the new Main Street that the city placed a small bronze plaque in the sidewalk near the Post Office to commemorate the event and to salute the thousands of "sidewalk engineers" whose contributions were "infinite" to say the least.

LIBRARY

The year 1963 marked the 100th Anniversary of Idaho's designation as a U.S. Territory. Governor Robert Smylie proclaimed that all Idaho cities should join in marking the year by developing a commemorative project. In search of an appropriate program, the City of Grangeville solicited suggestions. Ideas were plentiful but the request of City Librarian Marion Holt to build a new library was judged to have the greatest merit. The existing library was located in a cramped, airless room behind the City business offices.

After several weeks of deliberation by the Mayor and Council, a committee was appointed to foster the project. In a brochure published in 1974, on the tenth anniversary of the new library, members of the Grangeville Idaho Territorial Centennial Library told of the long meetings, night after night, followed by consultation with city officials, community groups, builders and architects. Sometimes encouraged, sometimes discouraged, but somehow always getting closer to the realization of the dream, the committee persisted.

Every member of the team, including Mrs. Joseph Montell, Mrs. Howard Higgins, Mrs. Bert Morris, Mrs. John Spencer, Jack Heartburg, Harold Smith, and Librarian Marion Holt, not only made personal calls to solicit funds but also took time to address civic clubs and other groups to gather support and new ideas. Mrs. Spencer told of the problem visualizing the actual size and dimension of the building from drawings. It was not until the entire floor plan was laid out full size with chalk on the floor of the Grangeville Armory that the team was satisfied with the space and design.

At first, it appeared that agreement on a suitable site for the building was impossible. Some insisted on a Main Street location. Others felt Main Street was too noisy for a library. The City offered a site at North State and West North Street that had been purchased years ago by a City Council with just such a purpose in mind. Considering the availability of parking, reduced traffic noise, and possibilities for expansion, the committee determined that this was the right site.

Funding for the building came from two sources; $26,500 was raised by private donations and $17,500 came from the federal Public Works Program. Holibough Construction Company, Greer, Idaho, was the successful bidder at $44,082. Accurate accounting of all donations and expenditures were the responsibility of the Library Building Fund Trustees consisting of Paul Eimers, Edward Brainard and Harriman Henry.

The Grangeville, Idaho, Territorial Centennial Library could never have been built without the support of the whole community — but the devotion and enthusiasm of those directly involved and their determination to get the job done was an inspiration to all!

POSTSCRIPT

More precious than gold are memories of life in Idaho County. While this is not a chronological account of the events spanning two decades, it is a story from the heart of some of the happenings that took place in the ordinary course of living. I hope it captures the character of the people and gives a taste of the time.

JAIL–BIRD–DOG

If the dog kingdom were a monarchy, Buck would be a Prince.

Good mannered, smart, handsome, probably a cross between a Shar-Pei and a Labrador, he was a dog of dignity and sensibility. If you like dogs, you would love Buck.

Yet, with all his virtues, Buck had a serious problem. This problem was his owner, a downright cantankerous, obstinate citizen named Malcolm Schwartz. Malcolm refused to confine his dog, allowing Buck free access to the entire Camas Prairie town where the elevation equaled the population (3,210).

Many unfortunate events occurred when Buck, on his daily *tour-de-promenade*, lingered too long at the home of a dog of the opposite sex or chased cats. Raving, angry citizens called the Mayor, the dog catcher, the police or all three.

"Come get this damn dog!"

"Why don't you enforce the Dog Ordinance?"

"If you don't get this dog right now, I'm going to shoot him."

Buck was not on everyone's welcome list.

After engaging in a number of unpleasant conversations with citizens complaining about Buck, the Mayor was heard to tell Joe Hartman, the dog catcher, "If you can't get Malcolm to keep that dog locked up, you catch him and put him in the pound or look for other work."

The sign says it all.

Later, the Mayor told the Chief of Police he regretted speaking so harshly to Joe Hartman, especially the part about looking for other work because he knew no one else in town would take the dog catching job.

Joe Hartman took no offense at the Mayor's intemperate words, knowing his job was secure. He was, however, more often allied with the dogs than the complainers. Resigned to enforcing the ordinance, Joe got lucky and caught Buck by speaking to the dog with kind words, inviting him to go for a ride in the city pickup.

Buck enjoyed the ride but found the City Pound much too confining. He moped around looking for a way out. He didn't have to wait long to make his escape. Malcolm Schwartz, in the cover of night, cut the chain-link fence releasing Buck and eleven other dogs.

The Mayor, the police and many citizens were upset by this turn of events. They talked about heavy criminal proceedings against Malcolm Schwartz for breaking and entering, trespassing, destruction of public property, aiding and abetting known vagrant unlicensed dogs.

After reviewing the facts of the incident, the City Attorney told the Mayor, "We can't prosecute unless we have proof. Up to now, you have only hearsay or thin circumstantial evidence. You'll have to catch Malcolm in the act of cutting the fence. Anyone could have cut the fence; eleven other unlicensed dogs escaped."

Joe Hartman continued to pick up the town's vagrant dogs, including Buck, depositing them in the City Pound. Buck hap-

Grangeville City Council, 1962. Left to Right: Mayor George Klein, Councilmen Harold Smith, Harriman Henry, Dick Large, Gene Olmsted, Glen Landreth and Don Ingram.

pily entered into the spirit of the caper — going for a ride in the city pickup, visiting with the other confined dogs, resting, eating, and waiting for Malcolm to spring him. Kind of a crazy game, but fun. Malcolm was very skillful at releasing the dogs and the city could not afford a round-the-clock watchman.

The City Fathers, in special session, unanimously approved the suggestion that Buck be incarcerated in the city jail.

"Good idea," said the Mayor. "Malcolm won't dare try to break into the jail."

No one thought to mention that the jail, in the basement of the city hall was never locked and was mostly occupied by drunks and vagrants during the annual July Rodeo Celebration.

The decision was made. Joe apprehended Buck and put him in the slammer. He did his time with repose and dignity. Except for an occasional bark or lonely howl, Buck was a model prisoner. There were some who said he was pampered, living on expensive dog food and tasty scraps from the Kandy Kitchen Cafe.

Each day, Police Chief Whitmore drove the prisoner out to the city dump where Buck exercised by chasing the varmints.

Everyone knew Buck was in the clink but nothing was heard from Malcolm until the sixth day of Buck's imprisonment. That day, the City Clerk was served by a summons and complaint from Malcolm Schwartz, plaintiff, naming the city as defendant and alleging that, "Said City did willfully, deliberately, deign to steal, restrain, incarcerate the plaintiff's male canine a/k/a Buck Schwartz. That Malcolm Schwartz, said plaintiff, claims real and punitive damages for irrevocable loss and suffering due to the acts of the defendant and hereby petitions the court that said plaintiff be granted $5,000 damages from said defendant."

The City Attorney immediately filed a countersuit citing a long list of grievances the city had sustained from Malcolm Schwartz as a result of his deliberate violation of the city and state laws. While Buck languished in jail, the attorneys pontificated and the press had a heyday.

Headlines blazed: "Bow Wow Behind Bars"; "Jailed Bird Dog Won't Talk"; "Buck May Beat System"; "Doggone In Jail!"

When sanity was finally restored, a compromise was negotiated. Buck was returned to Malcolm who promised to keep him confined. Buck, not having consented to the agreement, continued to escape. Now, however, he headed directly to City Hall where he insisted on being admitted to his old jail cell. Malcolm grumbled but came for his dog, time after time.

Buck would not give up. He continued to sprint for City Hall every time he managed to evade Malcolm. Finally, Malcolm called the Mayor and told him, "I've had it! You keep him."

It was no secret everyone at City Hall was pleased to have Buck. The Mayor and City Council chipped in to buy him a license and he was designated official City Dog. Occasionally, Buck got in trouble again but not often. He had arrived at the age where old dogs, having found a good home and reaching a certain station in their lives, finally mellow out.

DISCOVERY AT TOLO LAKE

On September 2, 1994, an amazing discovery took place at Tolo Lake, Idaho. Rich Gribble and Gerald Smith had pumped the small lake dry in preparation for the removal of the built-up sediment. Located five miles west of Grangeville, Tolo Lake is a popular recreation spot. The excavation work was part of a restoration project to improve fish habitat undertaken by the Idaho Fish and Game Department in cooperation with U. S. Natural Resource Conservation Service and local property owners.

When the heavy equipment unearthed a four-an-a-half-foot femur during removal of the sediment, State Archeologist Robert Hohe and other professionals from the Idaho State Historical Society were called to the scene. They identified the nearly complete remains of a huge Columbian mammoth, an elephant-like creature that became extinct more than 10,000 years ago.

Other bones, parts of some fourteen individual mammoths, also were found buried on the bottom of the lake.

The discovery of the mammoth bones generated a lot of excitement in Grangeville and throughout Idaho.

Tolo Lake always has been a subject of ancient lore as well as more recent history. Men and animals have gathered there for more than 11,000 years. Indians called it Te Pal-e-wam. Early settlers named it Tolo in honor of a Nez Perce woman, Tolo, who during the Indian War of 1877, risked her own life to summon

MAMMOTHS
DISCOVERED
AT
TOLO
LAKE

ON EXHIBIT APRIL 22-MAY 20
MONDAY-SATURDAY 9-5
IDAHO MUSEUM OF NATURAL HISTORY
IDAHO STATE UNIVERSITY

OPENING SATURDAY, APRIL 22, 7:00 PM
IDAHO MUSEUM OF NATURAL HISTORY
FEATURING
"THE MAMMOTH SITE OF HOT SPRINGS, SOUTH DAKOTA"
WITH
DR. LARRY AGENBROAD, PROFESSOR OF GEOLOGY
DIRECTOR OF THE QUATERNARY STUDIES PROGRAM
NORTHERN ARIZONA UNIVERSITY
AND
"PRELIMINARY WORK AT THE TOLO LAKE MAMMOTH SITE,
GRANGEVILLE, IDAHO"
WITH
DR. WILLIAM A. AKERSTEN, CURATOR OF PALEONTOLOGY,
IDAHO MUSEUM OF NATURAL HISTORY

Poster announcing the discovery of the mammoth fossils at Tolo Lake, Idaho.

Above: Allen Dedrow of the Idaho Museum of Natural History, Pocatello, Idaho, prepares the tusk of a mammoth elephant at Tolo Lake. Total length of the tusk, following its curve, is seven feet. Photo courtesy of the Idaho State Historical Society and the Idaho Museum of Natural History.

Left: A portrait of "Tolo." Right: Map shows location of Tolo Lake west of Grangeville. Courtesy Grangeville Chamber of Commerce.

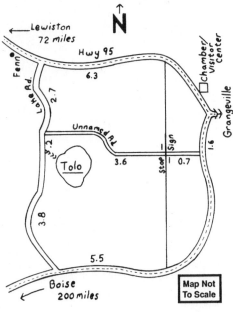

help for her white friends who were under assault by Indian warriors.

Excavation of an archaeological site is a slow and painstaking process. Many questions about the Tolo Lake mammoths are yet to be answered. Researchers want to learn more about the mammoths that gathered at the site and why many of them died there. It is possible that evidence of early man will be discovered at the site.

Local citizens have organized a group called "Friends of Tolo Lake" to raise funds toward the completion of the Lake restoration project and to resume archaeological exploration of the area.

Special Place

When someone mentions his own "special place," my mind goes to a wooded spot our family owned in the mountains about seven miles south of Grangeville, Idaho. Considering the wealth of scenic spots in the vicinity, my "special place" may not measure up to perfection but, to me, it is a place full of beauty and rich memories.

For many years, my wife Elvera and I and our three children made this our outdoor home. Sometimes we slept there under the trees, waking in the morning to watch the deer grazing just a few feet from our tent. Our son Bill was particularly fond of this "special place" and spent hours there, summer and winter, camping, skiing, and exploring for signs and relics along the Old Milner Trail.

Since moving to Boise, I frequently recall these memories. They are always associated with thoughts of Bill, a graduate of Grangeville High School and Gonzaga University and holding a Ph.D. from the University of Minnesota. Bill was killed in a car accident in 1968 when he was 26 years old. Some years ago, Elvera and I agreed that it would be appropriate to donate our land to the City of Grangeville in Bill's memory and to preserve the area for the people of Grangeville.

We hope this "special place" will be managed in a way that will retain its woodland character and that the timber will not

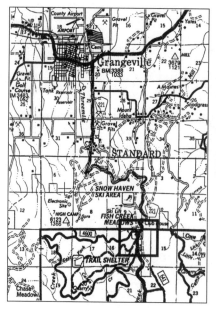

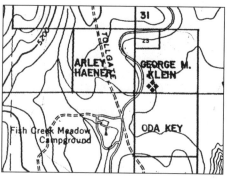

Location of the land donated by the Klein family south of Grangeville is shown in the box on the map at left. The location of the commemorative marker is indicated by the diamond in the detail of the map shown above.

The marker fronting the line of fir trees reads: "Grangeville Recreation Area. A gift to the City of Grangeville in memory of William M. Klein, Ph.D., 1941-1968." It can be seen from the Grangeville-Salmon River Road near Fish Creek Camp. (See maps, above)

be cut except to enhance the beauty of the area or for safety, appropriate recreation uses or historical denotation.

The history of the Old Milner Trail, which traverses this land, is a fascinating story. In her book, *Pioneer Days in Idaho County*, Sister Alfreda Eisonsohn records the picturesque past of the road leading to the gold mines at Florence, the first county seat of Idaho County. The late R. Ross Arnold, in a poem entitled "The Milner Trail," captures the mood of the wilderness route in these words:

> The feet which trod the old, old trail
> Have long since been at rest.
> Along its lonely reaches now
> The wild bird builds its nest.
>
> The wild syringa flaunts its bloom
> Across the Milner Trail.
> The wild deer's dainty footprints mark
> Its pathway through the vale.
>
> The silence of the drifting years
> Hangs heavy o'er it still
> Unbroken save by a calling bird
> Or a rippling mountain rill.
>
> Still memories haunt its winding path
> And crowd along the ways
> Of that uncounted multitude
> And those forgotten days.

We expect local persons or organization will advance appropriate and inventive plans for the use of this land by the citizens of Grangeville and others. Some of the uses we envision are: a historical and/or nature trail; an outdoor experience for scouts and campfire groups; a cross-country ski embarkation site; facilities for campers; a hikers' rendezvous for treks over the old trails into Florence and the Buffalo Hump Country.

With the wealth of adventure and romance to be found in our past, we may still find "gold in them hills" if we care to capitalize on our Idaho County's unique history. We love this county and its people and no matter where we happen to be in residence, we still live in Idaho County.

The "Starter"

In 1972, my wife Elvera published a small mimeographed booklet containing her favorite sourdough recipes. Elvera has a Bachelor of Science Degree in Home Economics from the University of Idaho and loves to cook. She is not a gourmet cook, she just prepares good, nutritious meals.

Yes, Elvera is a meticulous, serious creator of tasty, hearty, healthy, easily-digested food. She is ever mindful of number of calories, vitamins, and the danger of excessive fats. Her dishes are pleasing to the eye and a delight to the palate. Just thinking about her scrumptious meals activates the taste buds.

Elvera bakes equally as well as she cooks. People continually ask for her sourdough recipes: sourdough cinnamon rolls, pancakes, coffee rings, bread, waffles, and many more of her basic good, wholesome sourdough specialties. Elvera's little five-page mimeographed recipe book sold like hotcakes. All the proceeds went to the restoration of the organ at St. John's Cathedral in Boise.

Applauding the success of her little publication, Elvera's family and friends encouraged her to expand the book to include more of her sourdough recipes and directions for the production, handling and care of the perishable "starter." Elvera protested with various excuses:

"There are too many sourdough recipe books."

Elvera Klein. She has 39 different recipes in her book, Creative Sourdough Recipes, *published in 1987 and still popular. Photo courtesy of Boise State University, Albertson Library, Special Collections Department, and the* Idaho Statesman.

"I'm not a good writer and it's too much work."

"I just don't have time."

Finally, with continued urging and encouragement, she agreed to complete and publish a book of her sourdough recipes. She did not approach the job half-heartedly. Every recipe had to be tested and proven worthy. Elvera's kitchen became a bustling laboratory. The wonderful odor of fresh-baked sourdough victuals flooded the house. Of course, she had first- and second-opinion "tasters" who were eager to accommodate, thereby enhancing their waistlines, a fitting reward for their participation.

More than seventy sourdough recipes were tested and thirty-six were judged exceptional and qualified for inclusion in the publication. Following the judging, every recipe had to be checked for precise quantity of ingredients and exact baking instructions.

At this point, Elvera declared she was weary of the project but knowing that she had invented and perfected some fine foods in her kitchen laboratory, she began to organize the essential components for the book. There must be an introduction, illustrations and a suitable title; printing details had to be worked out.

Provocative decisions for the novice writer, these caused Elvera to be real "testy" at this stage of the production. There were those who opined that Elvera was suffering from "writer's block" or "author's blues." Writing the introduction kept her awake nights.

"It would be interesting to tell about Martin's experience with sourdough, don't you think?" she asked a friend as she stared at the blank sheet of paper before her. Martin Epeldi, a Basque acquaintance, had been a sheepherder in his youth. He had told Elvera of his solitary life and the perils of his lonely job. One of Martin's stories was about his sourdough "starter."

"I left my camp early and moved the sheep to better grass on the north slope," Martin recounted. "We got an unexpected strong wind and rainstorm and I had a bad time with the sheep. It was dark before I got the band settled down and I was dead tired when I got back to camp. I found the dang storm had just about blown the camp away. My sourdough starter was spilt on the ground but I scooped it up. You know, I saved only about a spoonful but it was enough to make a new batch. I was lucky. I couldn't have lived out there without that sourdough."

The friend told Elvera Martin's story was a good one but if she was going to write about the Basque Sheepherders, that could be the subject for another book.

"Not another book," Elvera protested. "I'm having enough trouble writing the introduction to this one."

Heeding the advice of her friends, Elvera relaxed and just put the introduction in her own words:

"The art of sourdough baking has been around for a long time, but the exact time it was discovered no one knows. The miners, sheepherders, farmers, trappers or anyone far from civilization depended on this living 'yeast' to make their breads, biscuits, and hotcakes. . . . I think you will find sourdough baking a creative and pleasant pastime."

"Creative Sourdough Recipes," Elvera thought. "That's a good title. Why didn't I think of that before? Now, I'm making progress."

The cover of Creative Sourdough Recipes, *by Elvera Klein. The cover art and numerous interior illustrations were created by Barbara Hamilton.*

Barbara Hamilton of Boise, a professional artist, designed the cover for the book and decorated the pages with forty illustrations, some of which were drawn from real baked models that Elvera had provided. The edible models were part of Barbara's compensation.

Creative Sourdough Recipes is an unpretentious little book of forty-one pages. Elvera is the sole author, publisher, and distributor. Sales in Idaho had reached about a thousand copies when she received a letter from Patricia "The Troll" McManus Gass, the sister of Patrick F. McManus, world renowned humorist and author, raised in Sandpoint, Idaho, and now living in Spokane, Washington.

Patricia wrote, "A friend has given me a copy of your great little recipe book. My brother Pat McManus and I are collaborating on writing a book combining memories of our Idaho childhood with recipes and commentaries. Would you consider permitting us to use some of your recipes in our new book? . . . ."

Elvera was delighted with the prospect of her recipes being printed on the pages of a popular and well-known author's book. The McManus book, *Whatchagot Stew,* published in 1989, contains twelve of Elvera's recipes as well as this generous compliment.

"Elvera Klein of Boise, Idaho, has elevated sourdough cooking to a major art form. Many of the following recipes have been pilfered from Elvera's *Creative Sourdough Recipes* which can be ordered directly from her. See Acknowledgments for address."

As a result of the recognition Elvera gained from the McManus book, she received orders and correspondence from throughout the United States and abroad. The following are a couple of samples from the stack of letters she has received:

"2/5/94
Dear Elvera:
    After 40 years of making sourdough pancakes I finally have <u>arrived</u>! We make your recipe exactly and <u>eureka</u>.

151

They were perfect. Thanks again. Even my dog 'Scout' wanted more, but we ate them all up.

Regards,
Zeke Smith
Yakima River Guide Service
Ellensburg, Washington

P.S. Picture of 'Scout' enclosed."

"2/5/92
Dear Mrs. Klein:

After trying out your recipes in Pat McManus' book "Whatchagot Stew" been meaning to order your book to try some more. Specially like those sourdough cinnamon rolls. Finally getting around to it (we're on `Bitterroot Time' over here—always late). Anyway, thanks.

I'm looking forward to trying more of your recipes. Please send to.

Doug Rohn
Florence, Montana"

Elvera was pleased that her book was a success but she dismissed the lavish praise and commendations as "overmuch." No, her publishing achievement did not spoil Elvera.

Occasionally a friend or family member teases her by calling her "Our Lady of Perpetual Sourdough" or makes some equally flippant remark but Elvera takes it with indulgence. She knows that with writing, as with sourdough baking, "It's the starter that counts."

THE ANONYMOUS VERDA BARNES

On January 21, 1971, Senator Frank Church's Administrative Assistant, Verda Barnes, flew from Washington, D. C., to Boise, Idaho, to invest me as the Senator's Idaho Field Representative. I was looking forward to our meeting.

Verda spent the first day of her visit in the inner office conversing on the telephone or talking to visitors. I was worried. Had she completely forgotten me?

Cleve Corlett, Church's Press Secretary, had accompanied Verda on the trip to Idaho. He had interviewed me immediately and composed a press release announcing my appointment. Cleve told me to relax. "You'll soon learn that Verda is one smart lady," he said. "I'm sure she has a reason for keeping you on hold."

Nevertheless, I was worried about my ability to function in what I perceived to be a loosely structured and haphazard organization. My experience in government agencies, my military service, and running my own business all had emphasized carefully defined duties and responsibilities. Earlier, I had expressed my concern to Senator Church. "Don't worry about that George," he said. "Verda will show you the way."

The following day, when Verda returned from her hairdresser, she invited me to join her for coffee at the Hotel Boise Coffee Shop. A large, circular booth at the front of the restaurant was the traditional site for the morning "Coffee Klatch" regularly attended by many of Boise's "important and influential" men.

Although Verda selected an isolated table, she was formally greeted by many of the Coffee Klatchers as they drifted in and out. The conversation at the "men's table" was sometimes loud and boisterous when there were hot arguments or when strong opinions were being pontificated. Conversely, it became very quiet when the heads bent close together to hear whispered accounts of a local scandal or an off-color story.

Verda enjoyed the give and take and the good-natured retorts exchanged between her and the men.

"Good to see you Verda. When is Frank going to get us a new post office?"

"Look out, Republicans. Verda Barnes is back in town!"

"Hi, Verda, how's the party of rum and rebellion?"

I was impressed. Not only did Verda know most of the greeters by their first name but she had an appropriate remark for each.

I rose to my feet each time she introduced me. "This is George Klein," she said "He is the Senator's new field 'rep.' He was State Director of the Farmers Home Administration . . . ."

I was worn out from popping up and down and shaking hands each time Verda introduced me. It was a relief when she powdered her nose and said, "Let's go, George. I'm having lunch with the Governor." I wondered when she was going to talk about the job.

Verda thought it overdone when, a few years later, a group of local militant women declared war on the male-only Coffee Klatch. They claimed the hotel management discriminated against women by catering to the male Klatchers. Organizing into assault teams, the women invaded the Coffee Shop before "drinking hours" and occupied the "men's" table. When the men arrived, they dispersed and shifted to other locations. After a few weeks, the women grew tired of the siege and abandoned the game. Some males cautiously commented, "No men, no fun!"

The Boise Hotel Coffee Shop is no more. But it is possible that even today, someplace in the heart of the city, the "Men Only

Perpetual Coffee Klatch" survives and prospers. I know Verda would still be a welcome participant.

Verda was a cigarette smoker and a moderate drinker of alcohol. She used them both for props — pausing to take a cigarette while formulating her thoughts on a controversial subject; sipping a drink as relief to listening to a boring conversation.

Verda's "special prop" was her compact. When she was irritated, impatient or simply weary of listening to nonsense, she took her compact from her ever-present purse, snapped it open, looked at herself in the little mirror, and powdered her nose. Sometimes she would put her hair in order; hair, now dyed a straw blonde, that was once a ravishing red. If she needed more time, Verda would return the compact to her purse and rouge her lips.

Verda was four years my senior but we had both experienced the great depression of the 1930s. We both were solid supporters of Franklin Roosevelt's New Deal. We had faith in his prescription for national economic recovery as stated in his address to the Nation in 1932:

> "This country needs and, unless I mistake it's temper, the country demands bold, persistent experimentation. . . . Take a method and try it. If it fails, admit it frankly and try another. But above all, try something. The millions who are in want will not stand by silently forever while the things to satisfy their need are within easy reach."

This accurately stated the condition and temper of the times. Perhaps it was political idealism but the enormous poverty and unemployment called for political action or anarchy and revolution. Subsequently, the streams of alphabet agencies were born: the Agricultural Adjustment Administration (AAA); the Commodity Credit Corporation (CCC); the Civilian Conservation Corps, (also CCC); the Resettlement Administration (RA); the Reconstruction Finance Corporation (RFC); the Works Progress Administration (WPA); the Soil Conservation Service (SCS); the National Youth Administration (NYA); and many more.

It was, as defined by Adlai Stevenson, Senator from Illinois and one-time United States Ambassador to the United Nations, "the great revolution of rising expectations!"

While Verda and I came from different backgrounds and life experiences, we and our families were engaged in the struggle for survival. Young and eager, we joined FDR's New Deal. Hardly out of her twenties, Verda went to work for the National Youth Administration. She shared their objectives of providing employment for youth from poor families and part-time jobs for needy students. With my brand-new Agriculture Degree from the University of Idaho, I was recruited to fight rural poverty and ease the hardships of low-income farms.

This simple poem may seem ludicrous today but it was not funny in the 1930s when it sincerely expressed the feeling of one poor family who received a rehabilitation loan from the Farm Security Administration.

Uncle Sam is my shepherd
And I shall not want.
He helped me to care for my children
And raise all my food if I don't.

He don't make me lie down in green pastures
He leadeth me down to the Tin Warehouse
And give me a cotton mattress.

He restoreth my cow and pigs
And some chickens and some eggs.
He leadeth me in the path of sleeping
When he gave me the cotton beds.

Yea, though I walk through the valley
And shadow of death to stay here
But as long as Uncle Sam hold everything
No evil will I fear.

Thou help me to prepare my table
It's a wonderful thing to tell.
Surely, the next few days of my life
On a government farm I will dwell.[1]

Verda was born and raised on the family farm at Wilford, a town no longer on the map because it was destroyed when the Teton Dam collapsed in 1976. Her father, John White, was a community farm leader and prominent in the Latter Day Saints Church. He was also active in the Democratic party. Verda was the second oldest of his eight children.

In 1926, the year Verda reached her seventeenth birthday, small rural Idaho towns were isolated culturally and geographically. There was great excitement and anticipation when a circus or carnival came to the area. The performers and even the carnival hacks, and roust-abouts were glamorous to young, pretty, naive country girls.

A carnival hand, a charming fellow named Jack Barnes, won Verda's heart and they were married. Jack stayed with her until their baby Valorie was born. But Jack was out of his element in the quiet country town, and he soon left it and Verda behind. Verda was devoted to her baby. With solid support from her family, she finished high school and for a short time attended Albion State Normal College.

It was a time when farmers throughout the nation were struggling to survive. Verda's parents still had six children on the farm to raise and educate. Best for all, Verda decided, to move to Boise and get a job so she and her child would not be a financial burden on anyone.

It was a "gutsy" move because jobs were scarce. Luckily, Verda found work with the Idaho Liquor Commission. She had to be resourceful to hold a job and also care for her child. The young working mother experienced all the financial and emotional problems of a single parent. Finally, Verda's mother, persuaded Verda to allow her to take care of Valorie temporarily.

---

[1] From *Poverty and Politics* by Sidney Baldwin, University of North Carolina Press, 1968.

Verda White Barnes, Director of the Women's Division, Political Action Committee, Congress of Industrial Organizations (CIO), circa 1938. Photo courtesy of Valorie Taylor.

I only recently learned of this trying time of Verda's life. It was a phase that she shared with few people. It was related to me by her dear friend, Myrna Sasser, who worked with Verda for more than twenty years.

Verda's friends and colleagues called her the "Redhead from Wilford," a live wire! She was good at her job, she reorganized Idaho's Young Democrats and was elected President, and she worked in campaigns for local, state and national Democrats.

Theodore Alexander Walters, an active Boise Democrat, was called to Washington to the job of Assistant Secretary of the Interior. He knew Verda and her capacity for work and her organizational ability. He asked her to join his staff. Verda accepted but it was a very traumatic and expensive move. Once in Washington, she was locked into the national political drama and never returned to live in Idaho.

Doors opened for the "politically moxie" woman from Idaho. Labor leaders Walter and Victor Reuther sought her advice on campaign techniques. She was a frequent invited guest to the White House where she joined Eleanor Roosevelt for tea and politics. A friend, Leon Henderson, WPA economist and labor leader, encouraged Verda to earn her degree in Economics at George Washington University. She did it after work and on weekends.

The demand for smart, capable staffers was great. Each new employer including Missouri's Senator Thomas Herrings and New Jersey Senator Harrison "Pete" Williams brought her new challenges and increased her knowledge. When Glen Taylor, "the singing Senator" from Idaho came to Washington he offered Verda a position on his staff and she accepted. Now, she could re-establish her ties with her native state.

Taylor lost his Senate seat to Republican Herman Welker in 1950 but Verda had no trouble finding work on "the Hill." When Frank Church was elected to the Senate from Idaho in 1956, Verda made it known she was available to serve on his Washington staff. Church acknowledged Verda's excellent qualifications but Glen Taylor had been hostile toward Church who had defeated him in the Primary Election. Verda's association with Taylor brought doubts about her ability to be loyal to Frank Church. Members of the Idaho Democratic Central Committee, led by Harry Wall of Lewiston, strongly endorsed Verda and vouched for her integrity. She got the job and was soon promoted to Administrative Assistant.

Verda's dedication to her job was notable but her enthusiasm for big league baseball was notorious. A fan of the Washington Senators, she demonstrated love for the game by her uninhibited cheering for her "Senator" on Griffin Field. The famous Home Run Slugger for the Senators, Harmon Killebrew, was from Payette, Idaho.

Home run slugger and Baseball Hall of Famer, Harmon Killebrew played for the Washington Senators.

Harmon, called "the Killer," hit 573 home runs and 1,584 base hits in his twenty-two-year career. Verda reveled in his glory. Harmon was inducted into Baseball's Hall of Fame in 1984.

It has been said that, "Pride goeth before destruction and haughty spirit." On one occasion, I gloated when I learned our Republican opponent had been embarrassed by poor attendance at campaign events.

"That will never happen on my watch," I boasted to Verda.

My wife Elvera, of Swedish descent, says, "You can identify the German characteristics in a person regardless of nationality. Whatever *you* do, they think *they* can do it better."

I tell her, "Please don't generalize. I know you are talking about me."

Just before Halloween one year, the program chairman of the newly chartered Karcher Mall Sunrise Lions Club invited Senator Church to be guest speaker. They met for breakfast at 7:00 a.m. every Wednesday at the Thoroughbred Restaurant on the mezzanine of the mall. Their first meeting fit our schedules and I was assured there would be a good turnout. The program chairman expected over seventy members and guests. Seven o'clock sounded incredibly early in the morning but it was campaign time. Where else could the Senator talk to seventy people at daybreak?

It was dark when we arrived at Karcher Mall in Nampa. There was no sign of life. I hadn't thought to ask how we were to gain entrance. The main door was locked. I was beginning to sense calamity. We separated and each rattled the pull bars on all the large glass doors. Finally, Bethine Church, the Senator's wife, found one that opened. We entered the dark central corridor, groped around until we found the lobby, then went up the stairway leading to the restaurant. When I saw the light at the head of the stairs, smelled the aroma of coffee and frying bacon, and heard voices originating from above, I told my sinking stomach, "It's going to be okay."

I proceeded up the stairs and into a large dining room. The place was empty except for five men huddled together at the far end next to the wall. The long white-clothed tables were set to accommodate at least eighty people. At each place there was a glass of orange juice, water, and yellow-and-black Halloween paper napkins. In the center of the tables were several round glass canisters of coffee, each perched over lighted candles keeping the brew hot and steaming. Miniature pumpkins were spaced between the coffee canisters.

All this, plus the black-and-orange streamers hanging from the light fixtures and the cutouts of ghosts and goblins on the walls, gave evidence that the restaurant had prepared well for a festive party. But five people! That was it! A stinging disappointment. I was ready to say "good-bye" and walk out but the Senator had more style. We stayed and had breakfast with the five who showed; then, standing, Frank Church gave a short talk:

"Several years ago, when Bethine and I first ran for the Senate, I was scheduled to speak at Fairfield, Idaho. It was miserable weather — then, we did not have George to manage our agenda." (The men turned to me and laughed.) "Consequently, no one showed up but one old cowman. He stayed, right there in the front seat, and I gave the rugged veteran of the range my splendid 35-minute speech. When I finished, I asked him if he had any comments. 'Just one,' he said, 'When I got a load of hay and just one critter shows up I don't drop the whole load!' Thank you all for coming."

Church stayed a while and answered their questions. The cattle story went over big; the Senator had told the yarn before but never to a sparser audience. The credit line to me was ad lib. I deserved it!

There were five messages on my desk when I returned to the office at 5:30 that afternoon; two were instructions to "call Verda." I dialed the Washington number. It was now 7:30 p.m. in D. C. and with any luck she would have already left. But she answered her phone.

"What happened at the mall this morning?" she asked.

I thought — She can't know already. But if she didn't, she

U.S. Senator Frank Church and his Administrative Assistant Verda Barnes at the home of George and Elvera Klein, Boise, Idaho, in August, 1977.

would have said "How did it go?" She must know. — So I blabbered all the sordid details and she made some very pointed comments.

I asked, "Verda, just out of curiosity, who told you about the breakfast at the mall?"

"You just did," she said. (I'm sure I heard a chuckle on the line.)

I often thought of Verda's salient remarks to me when we were alone once on the way to a fund raiser at Mountain Home.

"You know, George," she said, "being a United States Senator is a great job. The pay is generous and the perks are wonderful. Where else does your employer provide you with an in-house health spa, a parking space at the airport, and a staff of people to attend your official and personal needs. Plus there's the power and prestige that goes with the job."

Then she said, with emphasis, "The hard part of the job is getting elected and re-elected."

Verda's success was due in part to her skillful accumulation of information. She called it "Keeping my ear to the ground." Her principal tool was the telephone and her informants were everybody, everywhere. Many times, when I was on the road with Senator Church or advancing his agenda, my motel phone would ring at 6:00 a.m. Pacific Time or 7:00 a.m. Mountain Time.

"Good morning, this is Verda," As if I didn't know.

"What's going on out there?"

Or "How did it go last night?"

"Oh! Verda. Gee, it's awful early. Guess everything's O.K."

"They said you got lost on your way to the meeting." (How did she know?)

"Oh yeah, that. We were only twenty minutes late."

"Now, George, we have to plan better. No matter what the Boss says, you must get him to his appointments on time!"

It was uncanny how fast news traveled from rural Idaho to Washington, D. C. Sometimes the "Boss" and I felt that we were Verda's wayward children, off on an adventure in the wilds of Idaho.

Verda had a manner of responding to questions challenging her directives by alphabetically categorizing the answer; i.e., "A: It's cumbersome; B: It costs too much; and C: The Boss won't like it." The Boss?

Frank Church's wife Bethine and most of his relatives and intimate friends called him "Frosty." (Bethine says it caught on when a playmate who couldn't pronounce Frank called him something that sounded like "Frosty.") His staff, the press and most of his constituents called him "Senator." Verda Barnes called him "Boss." In "Verdamese," her reasons were:

A: It established the authoritative source of her orders; i.e., "Because the Boss says so."

B: It underscored her position as the Senator's subordinate and obedient servant; i.e., "I'm only following the Boss' orders."

C: It assured "the Boss" that she recognized his eminence and expected his strong backing; i.e., "Verda has to have my support to do the good job I expect of her."

I wasn't on the job very long before I witnessed how she "lit a fire" under "her troops." Verda usually flew out from Washington two days before the annual Jackson-Jefferson Day Banquet, the big Democratic event held each February. Upon arrival, she immediately contacted the Ticket Sales Committee Chairperson.

"How many tickets have you sold, dear?" she would ask.

"Oh, Verda, I'm so happy you're here. I don't have the exact count but it's somewhere between four hundred and five hundred."

"Four or five hundred! That's bad. You're going to have a half-empty house. We've got just eight hours to get a telephone bank set up to keep this banquet from being a disaster."

The poor volunteer chairperson was already sick and on the edge of a nervous breakdown.

"I don't feel a bit well, Verda. I think I'll have to go home."

"Nonsense, Sally, you just need some help. We'll all pitch in and make this the best attended J.J. ever."

The event was, as usual, crowded, noisy and exuberant! Tables had to be set up in the hall to take care of the overflow crowd.

One time, Verda forgot that the ticket sales chairman had experienced her "motivation tactics" in a previous year.

"Hey, Verda," he said, "you told me that in 1968 and we ended up with a standing-room-only crowd."

"Yes, that's true, Karl," was Verda's response, "but you would never have had the crowd if I hadn't alerted you to the problem. How many tickets did you say have been sold?"

I was beginning to get the drift — show and tell wasn't just a game for children. Verda's cardinal rules were: Whenever and wherever Senator Church was a guest or host, all seats must be filled. If the facility was too big for the size of the crowd, shrink it. If it could be expanded, fill it to overflowing. Make sure the acoustics were good and the sound system working. Then, get your big frame out of the way and keep your mouth shut.

An expert on grassroots campaigning, Verda stressed the following:

1. Concentrate your resources where you have a good chance to win votes. (Voter identification and door to door canvassing.)

2. Start early. Get exposure, TV time, sign boards, posters, press conferences, go anyplace you can get an invitation to speak.

3. Appoint wealthy and influential community opinion molders to your search and campaign committees. (Takes money to get money.)

4. Never believe polls or straw votes, particularly if they show you are in the lead.

5. Get your voters to the polls to vote.

Verda considered these to be vitally important and basic. Sometimes she improvised to fit new situations. Sometimes she got dramatic!

"I don't care if the polls say we are ahead twelve percentage points. I have very creditable information that we are trailing badly, perhaps by as many as 30,000 votes. We have to get some movement in Twin Falls County. Myrna, get those people out of the headquarters and out canvassing. I'll ask the Boss if he and Bethine will go over there Monday and work the mall and wherever else. George, be sure Bethine has a good supply of her little cookbooks and be sure she doesn't lose her purse."

In the spring of 1975, Elvera and I took our grandchildren, Steven, Laura and Richard, to Washington, D. C. In their early teens, they had never been far from their home in Hamilton, Montana. We stayed at Frank and Bethine's home in Bethesda, Maryland. They went all out to make sure the children had an exciting visit including a tour through the White House, lunch with the Senator in the Senate dining room, and a ferry boat ride on the Potomac River to Mount Vernon, George Washington's home and estate.

I was pleased when Bethine told me that Verda had phoned and invited all of us to her apartment for a buffet supper. Verda was a gracious hostess and she made a big hit with the children. She knew what sights appealed to them and she stimulated their interest in the District's history. Her own grandchildren, John and Carolyn, lived in nearby Bethesda with their parents, Valorie and George Taylor.

Verda's home in the Van Ness Apartment Building was light, well furnished and cozy. The outside walls were fifty percent glass windows framed by flowered drapes. I was reminded of the penthouse on the roof of the Boise Hotel that looked down only on the street and the tarred roofs. Verda's view was of the sky and the tops of a forest of deciduous trees that stretched for miles in two directions. I don't recall that anyone talked politics.

U.S. Secretary of the Interior and former Governor of Idaho Cecil D. Andrus; Idaho Governor John D. Evans; and U.S. Senator Frank Church, circa 1980.

It was a warm and friendly visit.

Verda's last visit to Idaho was in 1978. I was State Chairman of the Idaho Democratic Central Committee and our candidate, the incumbent Governor John Evans, needed help. Verda was supposedly retired but she volunteered to come out and lend a hand. The State Party provided her an office and a telephone line in the Idaho Building. Within three days, she had talked to every Democratic County Chairman, a third of the precinct committee people, most prominent Democrats in the State, and her own secret sources.

At the end of the five days, she announced her verdict. "This campaign is going nowhere. Your workers are completely pathetic or in sad disarray. You must get some spark in your organization or the Governor is going to go down in defeat!"

With that, Verda reached for her purse, took out her compact, looked at herself in that tiny mirror, and powdered her nose.

After a pause, she said, "George, you had better pass that word on to Jan Hammer." Jan was Evans' campaign manager.

U.S. Senator Frank Church with his first Administrative Assistant, Ward Hower, and Myrna Sasser, his last Administrative Assistant.

"I'm going across the street and talk to the Governor."

After several days of being cooped up in the tiny office, alone with the telephone, Verda and her faithful former lieutenant, Myrna Sasser, took off for her native land, the upper Snake River country, and various points en route. Thereafter, the tide began to turn and John Evans won the election to succeed himself as Governor of Idaho.

Other factors also led to the Evans victory but Verda's contribution was valiant. Not many knew at the time but she was not well and was experiencing serious suffering and pain. It was the "last hurrah" for Verda White Barnes, the woman who had worked in the shadow of her "Boss." She had so carefully protected her own anonymity that pictures of her were rare but few people have ever touched the lives of so many Idahoans.

In Leroy Ashby and Rod Gramer's book *Fighting the Odds: The Life of Senator Frank Church*, historian Ron Hatzenburcher was quoted as saying, "Verda Barnes' death in 1980 may have left a hole in Church's campaign staff that no one could ever fill."

I'm glad Verda never gave me a comprehensive, in-depth description of the duties and responsibilities of your average Idaho Field Representative. If she had (I'm sure she could not), I would probably have quit the job before I started and missed one of the greatest experiences of my life.

Verda's earthly remains are buried in the only remaining evidence of the town called Wilford, Idaho — the cemetery. But Verda Barnes lives in the memory of all who knew her.

Following is a partial transcript of a eulogy to Verda Barnes delivered by Frank Church at a memorial service for her in Washington, D. C., on June 17, 1980.

Four years later, the nation and the world would mourn the passing of this distinguished statesman and U.S. Senator from Idaho.

Remembering Verda Barnes

When Bill Hall, editorial page editor of the *Lewiston Tribune*, heard of Verda's passing, he sat down at his typewriter and wrote:

"They say Verda Barnes died in her sleep the other night . . . But that's preposterous. Verda Barnes never slept. Oh sure, she'd put on her gown and maybe lie down for a few hours the way ordinary people do, but it was only the campaign-worn body at ease. The mind never stopped. Year after indefatigable year, she would lie awake all through the night with that restless mind that was just made for politics churning out the nuts and bolts and the crisp daily stratagems of one Idaho political campaign after another.

"Died in her sleep? Don't be silly. No one who puts so much labor and thought into so many political causes could have had time for something as lazy and wasteful as sleep. And it showed. Verda Barnes was probably the most influential person in Idaho never elected to public office. From that vantage, she daily vacuumed Idaho for information on long distance telephone. She knew hundreds of people across the state. She kept constantly in touch, calling, calling, calling. Nothing that went on in Idaho, behind the scenes or otherwise, caught her by surprise. It was sometimes remarkable that, on more than one occasion, the first I heard of some new development here in Lewiston was through a call from Verda Barnes in distant Washington.

"Frequently, in recent years, including these last five years of her alleged retirement, she would leave Washington for a few months and pay the tithe of her time to the political party she believed in. She would

hole up in a Boise office and, without the title or the public appearance of anyone in charge, would take command of the frequently flagging Democratic campaigns.

"But it all took its toll. When she would leave Washington and return to Boise for those few months each campaign year, she really did function virtually without sleep. It was her nature and that of any sound politician to toss and turn half the night plotting the next day's moves, anticipating the opposition's thrusts and devising the counter-thrusts. But she found it increasingly difficult in recent years to adjust her time clock back to native Idaho. She would work into the evening, lie awake on into the night and then wake up in the morning on Washington time, which was about 4:00 a.m. in Idaho. And so on through another weary day.

"But no more. Her protegés were in place, the last ounce of energy was spent. So she died in her sleep they say."

It was nearly half a century ago when Verda Barnes arrived in Washington. The excitement and idealism of the New Deal drew her like a powerful magnetic to the nation's capital. The dynamic leadership of Franklin Roosevelt made a fierce Democrat of Verda. It brought her enthusiasm, ability and appetite for hard work and attracted the attention of the first family. Many were the times when this young woman from Idaho would slip in the back door of the White House and drink tea with her friend, Eleanor Roosevelt.

Over the next four decades, Verda Barnes worked for organized labor, for three other members of Congress, and for me. I was the luckiest for she worked for me the longest, 18 years, a dozen of which she served as my Administrative Assistant. All that time I had the pleasure of her company, the gift of her friendship, and the benefit of her advice.

"Jump at the chance, don't pass the seat up on the Committee on Aging," she once told me years ago when I was the youngest Senator. "You may not think that you're particularly interested in the problems of the elderly but you will find, as I have, that they grow more poignant with every passing year."

I took her advice and discovered that, as usual, she was right.

The secret of the extraordinary energy and dedication Verda Barnes brought to her work was not hard to uncover once you knew her. She genuinely cared about other people. She genuinely wanted to help them with their problems. Of course, that was her job, but it was the job she sought out for herself in life.

She took personal charge of any constituent problem brought to my office that could not be routinely solved. There were very few within our reach that she ever had to bring to me. It gave her special pleasure to find the illusive answer, to get results for the person in need, and then to give me all of the credit. . . .

. . . Verda Barnes possessed all the worthiest attributes; honesty, loyalty, compassion, industry, a refreshing pride in her country, state and party and her pioneer roots. In the long tradition of public servants, she deserves to be remembered among the very best. I never asked Verda about her religious beliefs, it would have been impertinent. Besides, it always seems to me that she sought fulfillment in the life she lived.

And so, I thought it might be fitting to close this all too brief remembrance with the words of Stephen Spender, those words he used in paying tribute to exceptional people like Verda Barnes:

Near the snow, near the sun, in the highest fields,
See how these names are fêted by the wavy grass
And by the streamers of white cloud
And whispers of wind in the listening sky.
The names of those who in their lives fought for life,
Who wore at their hearts the fire's centre.
Born of the sun, they traveled a short while toward the sun
And left the vivid air signed with their honour.

THE VINEYARD

Lou Daymyer was convinced that his piece of land near Nampa, Idaho, was the ideal site to realize his lifelong dream of owning a vineyard. The land was the site of a former garbage dump but it was located on a sunny slope, had an abundance of water, and sandy loam. Lou knew he could turn it into a thriving vineyard.

Never mind the doubters or the critics, he thought. What did they know?

Bill Clements, a wine grower who fancied himself an expert at growing grapes, may just as well have yelled down his wine vat instead of telling him, "Lou, this place is just too frosty for growing grapes. I suggest you plant Roman Beauty Apples."

"Who's talking about apples?" Lou protested. "Heck, Bill, anyone can grow Roman Beauty Apples. You'll see, this will be a productive vineyard."

Lou's optimism was partly due to his having read a recent encouraging article in the *Good Fruit Grower* on hardy seedless grapes. "Sweet with soft skins, new varieties including 'Intertocken' and 'Black Monukka' produce good fresh grapes, wine, or raisins," the article declared.

The writer's seductive prose continued: "Both varieties were developed by crossing selected European grapes with the native American hardy Concord. Horticulturists worked years to perfect these sweet seedless varieties, each with a slight pungent taste inherent to its Concord parent."

Lou's wife Anne read the article and reminded Lou of his promise to visit their daughter in California in the spring.

But Lou's enthusiasm for his vineyard project only increased after he read the *Good Fruit Grower* report. With happy anticipation he mailed his check for $847 to a nursery in Central Washington. He ordered 400 Black Monukka and 400 Intertocken barerooted, two-year-old vines to arrive on March 5, 1982.

Grapes grow on vines and vines need trellises made of sturdy posts and heavy wire. A mild winter allowed Lou to plow his field, set the 110 posts and string the 5,000 feet of wire that would be necessary. Completing the trellises took longer than he had anticipated and he was hard pressed to finish the job before the arrival of the vines.

Lou had obtained a number of good bulletins on the planting and culture of grapes from the County Agricultural Agent. He had learned there are more than 2,500 varieties including those developed from the native Concord. Although wine was made by our ancient ancestors long before grapes were cultivated, there are vineyards thriving today that are more than 500 years old. Lou was looking forward to taking his place in this centuries-long tradition.

The vines arrived and Lou was prepared to plant them without delay. He hired 17-year-old Frank DeLeon to help him. How interesting, Lou thought, that Frank could be a descendant of Ponce DeLeon, the Spanish explorer who sailed with Christopher Columbus and who discovered Florida while seeking the fabled "Fountain of Youth."

Yes, this was a good omen favoring the planting, Lou thought, the ancient vine, celebrated for divine powers, planted by a descendant of the seeker of the "Fountain of Youth." Lou was given to periods of fantasy.

Lou tried to explain to Frank his allusion to a possible ancestor but Frank said, "I don't know any Ponce DeLeon but I've got an uncle Pedro DeLeon."

Frank thought Lou was a little loco.

Threatening clouds notwithstanding, work continued on planting 650 grapevines on reclaimed land near Amity Road and Gray Lane, in Nampa, Idaho. All for naught. The site was subject to chronic late hard frost. Photo courtesy of Boise State University, Albertson Library, Special Collection Department, and The Idaho Statesman.

Lou and Frank worked every day from foggy morning to early darkness. They spaced the vines in rows at 8-foot intervals, digging deep, roomy holes for the roots. Their shovels sank easily into the sandy loam but punching through the patches of hardpan called for a heavy crowbar or sharp pick.

Digging 800 holes, one might think, should eventually unearth some geographical or historical artifact. But the there were no arrowheads or prehistoric fossils to be found. Lou was surprised, however, to find a live toad buried in the sandy loam about a foot below the surface. It was as large as his hand, a dirty brown color, and dormant.

Very strange, thought Lou, there are no ponds or live streams within a mile. Could this be another omen? But the prince who came under the spell of the bad witch was turned into a frog not a toad!

Examining the toad, Frank DeLeon said, "Boy, that's ugly. I'll smash it!"

He had raised his shovel ready to drive it down full force on the hibernating amphibian when Lou grabbed his arm.

"Let it be, Frank, it's not hurting anything. Lots of people eat those things and consider the legs delicious."

Lou wasn't really sure about toads but he knew people ate frog legs. The idea struck Frank as revolting.

As Lou reburied the toad, he wondered how it had managed to get that deep.

"A scientist may relate the depth of the hibernation to the severity of the winter," he told Frank.

In the late winter weather, the clouds were within a few feet of the ground. Canadian geese, returning to their night quarters at Lake Lowell after a day of foraging for food, flew through the heavy fog above them. Swooping low, concealed by the overcast, the squawking honkers trumpeted their wild and nomadic spirit.

Frank responded with the best imitation "honk, honk" he could muster. He told Lou, "My teacher told us they can fly about 50 miles an hour and they feed off the corn and grain fields within 100 miles in one day."

"I hope they don't develop a taste for grapes," Lou said with no real concern. "Two or three thousand geese could wipe out our crop in short order."

"That's dumb to worry about geese," replied Frank. "These vines won't have grapes for three years; besides, the geese will be far north when your grapes are ripe."

The two men had planted about 500 vines when a car stopped on the roadside next to the field. The driver got out and crawled through the barbed-wire fence. He said he was a photographer for *The Idaho Statesman* and asked if he could take Lou's picture.

"Sure," Lou said, enjoying the break. "What's the point?"

The young man explained, "My assignment is to take pictures illustrating 'Signs of Spring in the Country' but you are the only person I could find out-of-doors in this miserable weather."

Left: Reality in Reverse — Now that's what we call an apple!

Below: George Klein with the last of the apple crop. There ain't no more! What happened to the Big One?

Left: Roy Gipson babysitting the hired man's kids. Left to right: Able, Junior, and Blanca Farias.

The photographer took several shots and, sure enough, on the front page of the next day's paper was a picture of this old guy wearing his Renfro of the Mounties ear flap hat, bundled up beyond recognition, huddled over on his knees planting a grape vine. The scene was dominated by the heavy black clouds on a wind-driven, rainy, cold 15th of March, known to the Romans as the "Ides of March." If the caption had not spelled it out, no one would have known what Lou was planting.

The caption below the picture did not say, "This is the World's Greatest Grape Growing Authority at Work." Nevertheless, some people took it that way and, thereafter, many stopped to visit the vineyard-in-the-making and to ask questions of Lou.

"What kind of grapes?"

"Will you be making wine?"

"How do you prune grapes?"

"When will they ripen?"

"How do you get the vines to stay on the wires?"

Inspired by the publicity and in keeping with his new image, Lou responded to all questions with some wisdom and a lot of clever invention.

Frank, listening to Lou's dissertations, said "How come you say all that stuff? You never planted grapes before."

Lou chose not to dignify the remark with a reply.

Lou admitted he did not know everything about growing grapes but from the day they were planted, he did everything he knew for the good of the grapes. He fed, pruned, cultivated, watered and sprayed them. They were his dear children and he their loving provider and caretaker. Lou did not expect much of his new vines at first — only a modest 30 pounds per vine for a total of 22 tons of grapes.

It did not happen.

Well, maybe next year.

Each successive year, the failure of the vines to produce grapes was repeated. Long, vigorous, creeping vines with lush, green foliage appeared but few grapes.

In 1989, Lou picked 243 pounds of Intertockens. That spring, when a hard frost was predicted, he had covered several vines with sheets of clear plastic. Even for a few vines it was a tedious job, not practical for 800 vines.

Oh, Lou didn't blame the plants for not fulfilling his dream. They performed with vigor and precision. First, the primary buds, pregnant with fruit flowers promising a bountiful harvest, were coaxed out of their woody shields by the sun on a warm spring day. Unfortunately, they were destined to die when the thermostat inevitably dropped below F. 20 degrees.

Then, the vines, sensing the loss, activated the secondary fruit bud destined to be killed by another severe frost. Finally, the tertiary buds, charged with producing foliage and tendrils, were the sole survivors, developing into streamers of leafy canes reaching out 20 feet with strong, woody tendrils clutching the wire trellis.

Pitiful, fruitless, no-account vines. Lou was dejected.

"It's over," he said. "Eight years of failure and disappointment is enough!"

Lou's disaster was not comparable to one that occurred in 1988 when Roary Batrell, the crop duster, jettisoned 140 gallons of deadly herbicide over 10 acres of promising cherry crop, damaging the trees and spoiling the fruit. Roary claimed his insurance would reimburse for the damage but the company reneged on a technicality and Roary had to declare bankruptcy.

Lou was bitter about his own loss but he knew that he and the vines had done their best and the failure was not due to plant or human negligence.

Frank DeLeon left Idaho and went to work for the U.S. Immigration Service in New Mexico. Lou was glad that neither Frank nor Bill Clements, the wine maker who had warned him, were there to watch him tear up his vineyard and his dream. Not only did Lou hate to admit defeat, it was downright embarrassing for him.

A few weeks later, Lou ordered 105 Roman Beauty and 25 Golden Delicious apple trees.

To anyone who would listen he said, "Both varieties will grow into compact, sturdy trees capable of producing twice as many apples in less time than the old standard varieties!"

Lou was convinced that his apple trees would blossom over a long period; every year, they would produce a bountiful crop of rich-flavored, crisp apples on this ideal site on a sunny slope, favored by sandy loam, and with an abundance of water.

"Yes," he declared, "I'm sure this will be one of the most exceptional apple orchards in the State of Idaho!"

ABOUT THE AUTHOR

A native of Oakland, California, George M. Klein attended the University of Idaho, Moscow, and worked summers for the U. S. Forest Service. Following graduation in 1936, he was employed as Farm Management Supervisor for the Department of Agriculture.

He married Elvera Nelson and they had three children, Douglas, William and Mary Anne.

During the six years he spent in the U.S. Army during World War II, he saw action in both Europe and the South Pacific as an infantry officer. He left the Army with the rank of Lt. Colonel, returning to his duties with the Department of Agriculture at Moscow.

In 1948, he entered private business in Grangeville where he was owner-manager of the Credit Bureau of Idaho-Lewis Counties and president of the Empire Finance Corp.

During his tenure as Mayor of Grangeville from 1959 to 1966, a city library was built, Main Street was paved, the city-owned water system was expanded, and the first city planning and zoning ordinance was enacted.

In 1958, he became president of the North Idaho Chamber of Commerce and was one of the founders of the Clearwater Economic Development Association. He also was active for several years on the special committee to promote the establishment of the Nez Perce National Historic Park in Central Idaho.

In 1967, he was appointed State Director of the Farmers Home Administration and moved to Boise.

Named as field representative for U. S. Senator Frank Church in 1971, he retired from that position on November 1, 1977. The following year, he was elected State Chairman of the Idaho Democratic Central Committee. He volunteered to manage the Frank Church re-election campaign in 1980.

With a partner, he operated orchards in Canyon County for eight years. He is currently serving on the Advisory Board for the Frank Church Chair of Public Affairs at Boise State University.

DID YOU ENJOY THIS BOOK?
YOU CAN ORDER ADDITIONAL COPIES
DIRECT FROM LEGENDARY PUBLISHING.

*All proceeds from the sale of **The Nüremberg Fünnel** will be donated to the Grangeville Bicentennial Historical Museum.*

— ORDER FORM —

Name _____

Address _____

City _____

State _____ **Zip Code** _____

_____ Copies of The Nüremberg Fünnel @ $16.95 each $ _____

Add $2.50 for shipping for each book $ _____

Idaho residents add 5% Sales Tax $ _____

TOTAL: $ _____

Include check for total amount, or use credit card as indicated below:

❏ VISA   ❏ MasterCard   Credit Card No. _____

Signature _____ Expiration Date _____

To Order by Phone call: 1-800-358-1929
Quantity Orders Invited — Call for Bulk Pricing

To Order by Mail
Make checks payable to:
LEGENDARY PUBLISHING COMPANY
P.O. Box 7706
Boise, Idaho 83707-1706
U.S.A.

Please photocopy if additional forms are needed.